DRUMMERS COLLECTIVE SERIES

AFRO-CUBAN RHYTHMS FOR DRUMSET

By Frank Malabe
and Bob Weiner

Alfred Publishing Co., Inc.
16320 Roscoe Blvd., Suite 100
P.O. Box 10003
Van Nuys, CA 91410-0003
alfred.com

PUBLISHED BY ALFRED PUBLISHING CO., INC.
© 1990 MANHATTAN MUSIC, INC.

ISBN-10: 0-89724-574-1 (Book & CD)
ISBN-13: 978-0-89724-574-6 (Book & CD)

CONTENTS

KEY

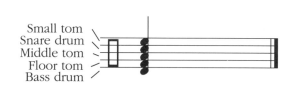

Small tom
Snare drum
Middle tom
Floor tom
Bass drum

Ⓡ/Ⓛ = rim shot

a. Cymbal or hi-hat with hand
b. Ride cymbal bell
c. Cowbell
d. Side of floor tom
e. Side of timbales
f. Hi-hat with foot

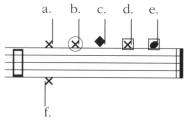

All other information not in the key can be found before each exercise. Optional notes are indicated by parentheses ( ).
Words appearing in **bold print** can be found in this book's Glossary.

FOREWORD

Afro-Cuban Rhythms for Drumset, by Frank Malabe and Bob Weiner, is an introduction to Afro-Cuban rhythms including the history, traditional instruments and basic styles of Afro-Cuban music. We explore the possibilities of adapting these rhythms to the drumset, an instrument which is not traditionally played in Afro-Cuban music. This book and cassette are part of a series that includes *Brazilian Rhythms for Drumset and New Orleans Rhythms for Drumset.* The material contained in all three books was developed over several years in a course called "Third World Rhythms for Drumset," which is taught at Drummers Collective in New York City.

Frank Malabe was born in New York City and began his professional playing career in the 1950's with the Angel Rene ... In the 1960's and '70's, Frank performed and recorded ... top Latin bands and bandleaders, including Pete Terrace, Tito Puente, Louie Ramirez, La Plata and La Playa Sextets, Willie Colon, The Alegre All-Stars, Tito Rodriguez, Celia Cruz, Jon Lucien, Bill Watrus, Johnny Pacheco, and Larry Harlow. Frank has recently worked and recorded with Charlie Palmieri, Dave Valentin, and Bob Mintzer, as well as playing Afro-Cuban folkloric music with the group Patakin. In addition, Frank is an instructor at the Harbor Performing Arts Center and at Drummers Collective in New York, where he teaches conga and the creative possibilities of Afro-Cuban rhythms as applied to drumset. Frank has also given master classes at the Eastman School of Music, and in the town of Bahia in Brazil.

Bob Weiner has played many styles of music as a free-lance drummer, including folk, funk, fusion, jazz and big band, as well as African, Caribbean, Jewish and Middle Eastern music. Working with Harry Belafonte from 1981 to 1986, Bob gained experience and exposure playing traditional calypso, Brazilian, reggae, African, and gospel music. Bob has also worked with the popular South African singer Letta Mbulu, American jazz singer Dianne Reeves, and Caribbean singer Jon Lucien, as well as Hugh Masakela, Herbie Mann and The Andy Statman Klezmer Orchestra. Bob organized the "Third World Rhythms for Drumset" course at Drummers Collective in 1984.

The cassette tape is the focal point of this project. At first listen, try to get a feel for the instruments and rhythmic phrasing. An exercise number and introduction is given before each exercise on the tape. These *audio cues* correspond to the information in the gray boxes before each example in the book. You may want to write in specific tape cues corresponding to the counter on your cassette player in the major sections of the book (or before each exercise) to help you reference the tape quickly. Due to the large number of musical examples included on the tape, most of the exercises are not long enough to play along with. We felt that it was more important to provide as many examples as possible to introduce the many different rhythms and styles of Afro-Cuban music.

The topics covered in Sections 1 through 4 include the Afro-Cuban 6/8 feel, different clave patterns, palito, cascara, and bell patterns, all of which form the foundation of the rhythms that follow. Sections 5 through 9 cover the rhythms *guaguanco, conga, mozambique, songo* and *merengue*. The rhythms are played in their traditional form and then adapted to the drumset. Section 10 contains two patterns by Frank Malabe that are derived from various Afro-Cuban rhythms and arranged for two drumsets. The tape concludes with a medley of different rhythms from the book played on both conga and drumset. The first time through features clave, conga and drumset and the second time only conga and clave so that you can play drumset along with the tape. We suggest that you progress slowly through each section, carefully studying the material. There is a lot of information here and taking it step by step will prove worthwhile.

These rhythms are part of a living musical tradition. Seeing and hearing where they belong in the music is essential. Recordings can help tremendously; seeing live performance is even better. We've listed an extensive discography in the back of the book with suggested recordings in the different areas of Afro-Cuban folkloric and popular music. The introduction, bibliography and glossary will help explain this unique and rich musical tradition.

ACKNOWLEDGEMENTS

The musical examples on the tape were played by the following:

Louis Bauzo   Tumbadora (conga drum), Bell, Shekere
Frank Malabe   Tumbadora, Drumset, Bell
Michael Spiro   Tumbadora, Shekere, Palito
Bob Weiner   Drumset, Timbales, Bell, Clave
Recorded at Dessau Studios, N.Y.C. Engineered by Drew Vogelman and David Sardi. Remixed by Doug Epstein.

We would like to express our gratitude to the following people for their invaluable help in preparing this book: Louis Bauzo and Ramon Rodriguez from the Harbor Performing Arts Center for their cooperation and help with the historical aspects of this book; Ken Gumbs and Dan Dawson from the Caribbean Cultural Center who provided us with many of the photographs; John Gray for compiling the bibliography; John Riley for his ideas and help with the musical transcriptions; Tony Martucci for giving the musical examples a "test run;" Rene Lopez, for help with the discography; Jacqui Russell, for editorial assistance and English-language "judgment calls;" Ellen Forney, who painstakingly typed and corrected the original manuscript; and a very special thanks to Rob Wallis and Paul Siegel for their support and funding of this project, allowing us to publish a book of this quality. Last, we would like to thank Jack Waltrip, Emily Moorefield, and Dan Thress for their commitment and dedication, without which this book would not have come to completion. The generous cooperation of all these people made *Afro-Cuban Rhythms for Drumset* a reality.

Frank Malabe and Bob Weiner

Frank Malabe would like to dedicate this book to Anthony, Yvette, and Rio.

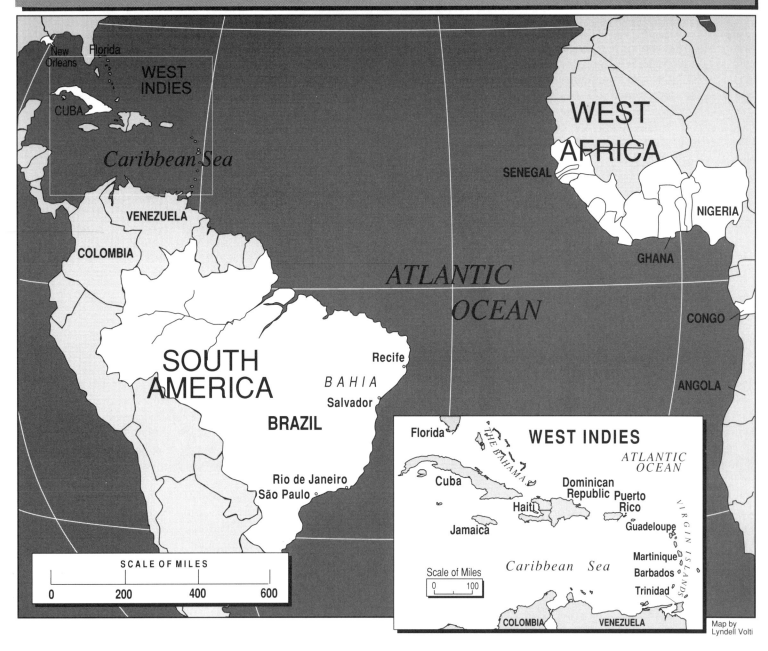

Map by
Lyndell Volti

Throughout history as people have migrated around the world their culture, including their music, has mixed with that of others to create new musical forms. In the United States, South America, and the Caribbean, the influence of African rhythms is particularly strong. Rock, R&B, jazz (United States), bossa nova, samba (Brazil), salsa (Cuba, Puerto Rico, New York City), reggae (Jamaica) and calypso (Trinidad) all have African rhythmic origins. To account for this, we must look at the common history of the regions where these forms first began to develop.

The islands of the West Indies were among the first areas of the New World to be colonized by the great European powers—Spain, Portugal, England and France. Originally inhabited by various Indian tribes, they were taken over in a manner that is by now well-known: Indian populations were enslaved or eliminated until the Europeans gained control of the areas they wanted and began exploiting agricultural and mineral wealth. To turn such "undeveloped" lands into moneymaking enterprises required huge amounts of cheap labor. In those days in the Americas, that need was filled by the African slave trade. Slavery brought hundreds of thousands of Africans to the Caribbean islands, South America, and the United States. Most came from West Africa, though many were also taken from central Africa, the region now known as Zaire. Portugal shipped slaves from its colonies Mozambique and Angola in southern Africa to its New World settlement, Brazil.

From the 17th to the 20th century in the colonized regions, Europeans, Africans, and what was left of the Indian populations came together in an immense blending of race, language, religion, social customs—and of course, music. Drumming is an integral part of everyday life in Africa, and the traditions from there were carried on in the Caribbean and Brazil. Music and dance are central in these societies to religious and social ritual, communication, and entertainment. Drums are believed to have spiritual power, power to heal, to "speak," to tap natural forces and affect human energy and emotion. The styles mentioned earlier all use African rhythms and European-derived melodies, and instruments from both cultures.

In Cuba, Puerto Rico, and the Dominican Republic, the mixture of African rhythms and Spanish music led to new forms which have recently come to be called *Afro-Caribbean music.* Since the majority of the rhythms discussed in this book are from the Cuban musical tradition, we will be using the term "Afro-Cuban." A closer look at the regions mentioned will help to explain the evolution of this music.

CUBA
The name Cuba comes from the Indian word *cubanacan,* meaning "center place." It is the largest island in the Caribbean. Cuba's first inhabitants were Indians of two tribes, the Tainos and Caribs. Both were all but annihilated by the

Spanish, although traces of Taino culture remained.

Under Spain, Cuba became the most profitable sugar-producing region of the world. Sugar was an enormously valuable commodity in the 17th and 18th centuries; individual fortunes and national economies were founded on the sugar trade. Thousands of African slaves were brought in to work the vast cane plantations. These slaves were controlled by the Spanish in various ways. Among other things, they were forced to speak Spanish and to accept Christianity. In defiance, slaves gave their African gods the names of Christian saints and continued to worship them in their native languages. This form of worship, known as *Santeria*, preserved many African religious, ritual and musical traditions, and is still practiced today. Santeria is the Yoruba religion from Nigeria, as it has survived in Cuba. In its ceremonies we can hear West African rhythms in their nearly-original state. The hourglass-shaped *bata* drum is used in Santeria to contact the *orichas* (deities believed to represent and control the forces of nature).

The merging of African and Spanish influences resulted in many new forms; one of the most important is the *son*. Son is the root of most familiar styles of Afro-Cuban dance music. It is believed to have originated in Oriente, the eastern province of Cuba, toward the end of the 19th century, and was a blend of the music of the *campesinos*, or farmers of Spanish descent, and the African slaves (slavery was not abolished in Cuba until 1878). It was played by small bands, using guitar or *tres* (a guitar-like instrument with 3 sets of strings) from the Spanish tradition; *maracas, guiro, claves* and *bongos* for rhythm; and for the bass parts, a *marimbula* or African "thumb piano" (a large version of the kalimba) which the player sat upon, and the *botija*, a clay jug with a hole into which the player blew to produce low notes. By the turn of the century, son was being played in Havana, taking on a more urban character and growing more and more popular, finally becoming a national style in the 1920s.

The best-known son band of the '20s was the Sexteto Habanero. This group replaced the marimbula and botija with the string bass and added the trumpet. The Septeto Nacional of Ignacio Piniero in the late '20s carried these innovations further: their tighter sound, faster tempos, and simpler rhythms emphasized the Spanish aspect of son more than the African, while the trumpet added a distinctly urban flavor.

Son was revolutionized in the late '30s by Arsenio Rodriguez, the great blind Cuban tres player. By enlarging the son *conjunto* (band) to include *tumbadora* (conga drum), cowbell, piano, and two additional trumpets, he brought much of the original African influence back into son while at the same time expanding on the form. Rodriguez modified son in a number of important ways. The *estribillo* section (a vamp using call-and-response) became a full-blown *montuno* or *mambo* section, with heavy rhythms to back up solos; this later gave rise to the dance we know as the mambo. There was greater use of and adherence to the clave rhythm throughout the music. *Tumbao* was developed—repeating phrases played by the bass and conga. The *guaguanco*, Cuba's most popular rumba form, was worked into the son style, and the tres became more important as a solo instrument.

The Cuban son would provide the basis for the Latin jazz styles of the 1940s, the popular dance orchestras of Machito, Tito Puente and Tito Rodriguez in the '50s, and the tipico and salsa bands that began in the '60s and continue to the present. In addition, such great musicians as Chano Pozo, Celia Cruz, Mongo Santamaria, and "Patato" Valdez helped bring Cuban styles to a place of international importance.

Other styles of music were popular in Cuba while son was developing. Most of this was dance music of European descent which was played by small versions of European orchestras. These groups, known as *orquestras tipicas*, performed the dance music fashionable with the Cuban upper class of the late 19th and early 20th centuries. Such dances as the *habanera, ritmo de tango* and *contradanza* were well-known in Cuba; the *danzon*, a 19th-century variation on the contradanza, was also a favorite, and in its later forms was very influential upon Cuban popular music.

Smaller versions of the orquestras tipicas, called *charangas*, also grew out of the contradanza tradition. Using violins, piano, flute, upright bass, *guiro*, and *timbales* (a Latin adaptation of European kettle-drums), the charanga became a basic component of Cuban music. Charangas of the 1950s developed and popularized the *cha-cha-cha*, one of the many Latin "dance crazes" of the post-war era.

PUERTO RICO

Called *Boriquen* by its first inhabitants, the Taino Indians, Puerto Rico ("rich port" in Spanish) is a small island east of both Cuba and Hispaniola (Haiti/Dominican Republic). It was a colony of Spain until 1898, when it declared its independence; the following year, after the Spanish-American war, Puerto Rico was made a colony of the United States.

Historically there has been a greater gap between the upper and lower classes in Puerto Rico than in the rest of the Caribbean. Although slavery was abolished in 1835, racism was not: most blacks remained at the lowest levels of Puerto Rican society, while the upper classes tended to be whites of Spanish descent. Races and cultures still intermingled, but the distinctions were clearer than elsewhere. We can see this division in the earlier forms of Puerto Rican music, which tend to be either mostly Spanish (*danza, decima, mapeye, aquinaldo*) or mostly African (*bomba, plena*). Even though there are many variations, the generic term "bomba" was applied to all African-derived music in Puerto Rico.

Bomba is a specific style, however—a Puerto Rican folk dance music which draws heavily on African tradition. It uses three drums, one of which, the "lead," improvises on top and keeps the dance moving while the other two provide a steady rhythm underneath. The bomba is a repeating pattern, with a counter-rhythm usually played on the side of one of the drums. It is still performed as part of the Santiago Apostol festival in the town of Loiza Aldea in Puerto Rico, a center of African musical tradition.

Bomba was first adapted for the dance band in 1957 by Rafael Cortijo, a Puerto Rican percussionist. His band Cortijo y Su Combo, fronted by the extraordinary singer Ismael Rivera, succeeded in updating the bomba without losing its folk appeal, its African roots—or the Latin audience, who demanded authenticity in their music.

The *plena* is an Afro-Puerto Rican song form that has long been popular in Puerto Rico among both blacks and whites. A plena consists of a verse of 4 to 6 lines and a chorus, and is usually a satirical or humorous look at current politics or social conditions. Various instrumentations have been used, from simple percussion and guitars to full dance bands. The best-known plena musician was singer/composer Manuel Jiminez, "El Canario," whose songs often dealt specifically with the concerns of people living in *El Barrio* (Spanish Harlem). Mon Rivera was also a famous plena singer. The Cesar Concepcion band, one of the top Latin bands of the 1940s and '50s, combined the plena tradition with big-band music in a way that was especially appealing to American audiences.

While the bomba and plena represent important developments, Puerto Rican music on the whole has not had as widespread an influence as Cuban. However, many great Puerto Rican musicians—composer and bandleader Rafael Hernandez, trombonist Juan Tizol (known for his work with Duke Ellington) and pianist Noro Morales, to name but a few—have played a major part in the development of Latin music from within, and in the spread of these styles to the non-Latin world.

THE DOMINICAN REPUBLIC

The Dominican Republic lies on the eastern half of the island called Hispaniola or Santo Domingo, between Cuba and Puerto Rico. Haiti, a former French colony, occupies the western half. It was first inhabited by Taino and Carib Indians, whose name for the island was *Quisquella*. The Dominican Republic declared its independence in 1844 although, as elsewhere in the Caribbean, the influence of Spain and later the U.S. was prevalent in their society.

Though the same blending of African and European traditions occurred, the results were very different than in Cuba or Puerto Rico. Generally, Dominican music and dance styles tend to be regional, thus keeping more of their original form. By far the best-known of these Dominican country styles is the *merengue*.

Merengue is a quick 2/4-time dance music that developed in the early 19th century. It was probably the result of French (Haitian) influence, as the 2/4 rhythm is common to much French folk music, from the old *contredanse* (French version of contradanza) to the later polka. The first merengue groups used the accordion, *tambora* (a double-headed drum played with a stick and muted with one hand), and *guira*, a metal guiro peculiar to Dominican music. A *cinquillo,* or fast-paced five-beat accent, was also characteristic of the form. Modern merengue bands have added horn sections and increased the tempos, but the basic elements remain unchanged.

Angel Viloria's band popularized the merengue in New York City during the 1950s. The singer Dioris Valladares got his start with this band, as did tambora player Luis Quintero. Both helped move the merengue style into the mainstream of Latin music. More recently, Johnny Ventura, Millie y los Vecinos, and Wilfrido Vargas have renewed its appeal with their modern instrumentation and choreography. The merengue grew in popularity throughout the '70s and '80s, due to the greater number of Dominican immigrants in New York, and is now an important part of the Latin music scene.

AFRO-CUBAN MUSIC IN THE UNITED STATES

In the 1920s, when Puerto Ricans first started coming to the United States in large numbers, they brought Cuban styles as well as their own folk music with them. Many settled in New York's East Harlem, a neighborhood that would come to be known as El Barrio. El Barrio played a vital role in the development of Afro-Cuban music, serving as both a haven for traditional musical forms and the spawning-ground for nearly every new development

Cuban music came to widespread attention in the 1930s with "The Peanut Vendor" ("El Manicero") by Don Azpiazu and his Havana Casino Orchestra. "The Peanut Vendor" was a type of son called a *pregon*, adapted from the songs of Havana street vendors. Azpiazu toured the U.S., and many new Latin bands were formed as a result. The rumba craze (popularity of the dance called the rumba) that followed the success of "The Peanut Vendor" saw the rise of Latin groups, such as the well-known Xavier Cugat Orchestra, that catered to downtown (i.e., non-Hispanic) audiences. At the same time, other bands were playing a more genuine Latin music with the uptown (Latin/El Barrio) audience in mind.

Many Latin musicians of the '30s also tried "crossing over" into jazz, and vice versa. Juan Tizol's "Caravan," composed for Duke Ellington, and Cab Calloway's "Minnie the Moocher" and "The Congo-Conga" are good examples of this sort of hybrid. The brilliant Cuban arranger Mario Bauza worked with Chick Webb and Cab Calloway during this period. Bauza's ideas would be extremely influential in bringing a new jazz sound to Afro-Cuban music, especially in the horn arrangements.

The appearance of Machito and his Afro-Cubans in 1940 was a major musical event. This group was composed of a powerful rhythm section including piano, bass, bongo and timbales, coupled with trumpets and saxophones playing jazz harmonies. Machito (Frank Grillo), lead singer Graciela (his sister), and the Afro-Cubans, with Mario Bauza as musical director, revolutionized Latin music by combining these forms. They were the inspiration for the major innovations of Latin music in the 1940s: the mambo and Latin/jazz.

The mambo, another dance craze that helped bring Afro-Cuban music into the mainstream of American culture, was originally the "shout" (also called montuno or mambo) section of son music, in which patterns are repeated. It can be an especially exciting part of the music; as played by Machito's band, it rarely failed to get the crowd up and moving. Dancing in the mambo section quickly became the rage, and the mambo as we know it was born. At the forefront of the New York mambo movement was Jose Curbelo's group. Two of his musicians, singer Tito Rodriguez and timbalero Tito Puente, went on to form two of the most important Latin orchestras of the 1950s.

Latin/jazz, also called "Cubop," was the result of the blending of "be-bop" jazz with Afro-Cuban rhythms and instruments. Dizzy Gillespie's concert at Carnegie Hall in 1947 and Stan Kenton's recording of "The Peanut Vendor" that same year signalled the arrival of the new form. Gillespie's Carnegie Hall show introduced the great conguero Chano Pozo, one of the first of many musicians rooted in authentic Afro-Cuban tradition who would become known to a much wider audience. Stan Kenton continued to experiment with Afro-Cuban and Brazilian music in his big band, and Machito worked with many of the great jazz soloists of the day. Latin/jazz continued in the 1950s with notable work by Cal Tjader, whose band included percussionists Willie Bobo, Armando Peraza, and Mongo Santamaria (an important leader in Latin/jazz from the 1960s to the present).

Mambo remained popular through the '50s; in addition, a new dance craze began—the cha-cha-cha. Popularized first in Cuba by the Orquesta Aragon, a flute-and-violin charanga, the cha-cha-cha quickly became popular with both Latins and non-Latins. Although some bands played a more authentic cha-cha-cha—including Machito, Tito Puente, and Tito Rodriguez, with their shows at the famous Palladium Dance Hall in New York—the majority produced extremely commercial versions. The diluted versions of the cha-cha-cha ended up reinforcing the image that most Americans still had of Latin music as a non-serious form.

Wary of the trivializing effect of mass-market appeal, many Latin musicians began looking to less well-known forms to experiment with. The '50s saw the growth of the merengue as well as a renewed interest in the plena style (Mon Rivera, Rafael Cortijo, Moncho Lena).

Charlie Palmieri's Charanga Duboney kicked off the '60s, debuting on New Year's Eve. They were an immediate hit and set off a "charanga craze" in New York. Dozens of charangas sprang up over the next several years, playing the *pachanga*, a fast and energetic dance. Conga players Ray Barretto and Mongo Santamaria both formed popular charangas. By mid-decade, however, the charangas were being replaced by the "old-fashioned" or *tipico* sound. "Tipico" is the root or folk form of any musical style. In trying to recapture the feel of an earlier era, many of the new bands of the '60s adopted the instrumentation of the old son conjuntos of the '20s and '30s. Flutist Johnny Pacheco, a founding member of Charanga Duboney, formed a very successful group which served as a school for new talent. New bandleaders such as Ray Barretto, Eddie Palmieri and Larry Harlow extended the range of their orchestras to include the tipico style. These "tipico extension bands" had a traditional yet hard-hitting, modern sound that laid the groundwork for the salsa music of today.

The "descargas" or jam sessions which took place in the '60s marked another important merger of Latin and jazz. These were composed of groups of musicians recorded by the larger Latin labels and featuring the musicians as the "Alegre All-Stars," "Fania All-Stars," etc. More informal and improvisational than Cubop of the '40s and '50s, the descargas gave many of the greats of New York Latin music a chance to play together and to "stretch out" on the music. The Alegre label was also the first to give individual musicians credit on albums for the instruments they played.

In the 1970s, the word *salsa* came into use to describe the popular Latin-hybrid music of New York. Salsa (Spanish for sauce, especially a hot and spicy sauce) is not a type of rhythm but a nickname for the music itself. This style has already seen many changes and interpretations. There is a "traditionalist" following that favors a rougher, "street" sound and lyrics dealing with everyday-life situations; and there are fans of the commercial sound with its romantic lyrics and singing. There are also those who prefer a more "progressive," jazz-influenced approach. Eddie Palmieri is one of the most influential musicians in this category performing today.

On the whole, most of the important advancements of Afro-Cuban music in the 1980s took place in Cuba, where bands such as Los Van Van continue to innovate. One development that is now beginning to catch on in the U.S. is the *songo,* which came about in Cuba in the late '60s. The songo, a rhythm developed by the percussionist Jose Quintana (Changuito) of Los Van Van on both congas and drumset, has had a great influence particularly among jazz and Latin drummers in the 1980s. Although some non-Latin players have integrated it into jazz, fusion, and other popular styles, the main band to work extensively with songo patterns in the U.S. has been the Puerto Rican group Batacumbele. As Latin music in America moves into the '90s, it is probable that not only individual players but the musical commmunity as a whole will again open up to the free-spirited creativity that has for decades been the mainstay of Afro-Cuban music.

SECTION 1

AFRO-CUBAN 6/8 FEEL—BEMBE, FOLKLORIC FEEL

Some of the fundamental rhythms in West Africa are based on 6/8 feels. In Cuba, one popular 6/8 feel is known as **bembe,** originating from the word *bembes,* which are religious gatherings that include drumming, singing and dancing.

Let's listen to an example of the Afro-Cuban 6/8 feel played in a folkloric setting. This example is played on a *hoe blade, shekeres* (hollowed-out gourds with beads loosely wrapped around them), and *conga drums* (tumbadoras). This feel, played in Cuba, is completely African in style and instrumentation. Similar rhythms are heard throughout West Africa, especially in Nigeria (the Yoruba tribes) where much of the African population in Cuba originated. You'll hear the entire feel, and then each instrument solo, to show how the individual parts interlock.

SECTION 1, Afro-Cuban 6/8 feel, Bembe (folkloric feel)

Hoe Blade

Low Drum

High Drum

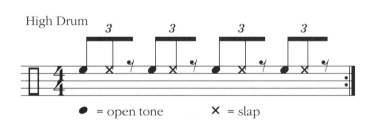

● = open tone   ✕ = slap

Shekere 1

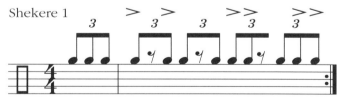

＞ = hitting the base of the   shekere

Middle Drum

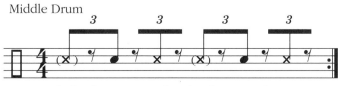

(✕) = bass note with palm down on drum

Shekere 2

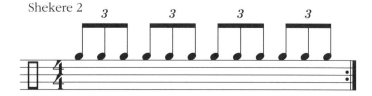

6/8 CLAVE PATTERN

It's essential to understand the importance of **clave** in Afro-Cuban music. Clave is a Spanish word meaning "key." The clave is the key to the rhythm being played, serving as a skeletal rhythmic figure around which the different drums and percussion instruments are played.

Any rhythmic figure can serve as a clave. We will be using what have become the most popular and important claves in African and Afro-Cuban music.

The clave rhythm is typically played on an instrument called **claves**, two round, solid pieces of wood which are struck one against the other. Clave figures can also be played by clapping your hands, hitting your drumsticks together, playing a cross stick on the snare drum or striking the side of the floor tom. Claves are used in Afro-Cuban folkloric and dance music, but are not usually played in Afro-Cuban 6/8 feels. We are playing the 6/8 clave only to show how it relates to the 6/8 cowbell pattern.

Exercise 1   6/8 clave counted in 6/8 time

Exercise 2   6/8 clave in 4/4 time, with triplets

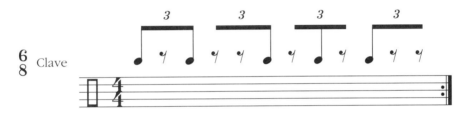

Now play quarter-notes on the hi-hat with your foot along with the 6/8 clave figure, while counting eighth-note triplets.

Exercise 3   6/8 clave counted in 4/4 time, with hi-hat on quarter-notes

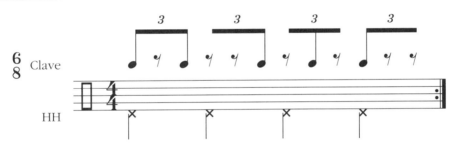

6/8 Cowbell pattern

The 6/8 cowbell pattern corresponding to the 6/8 clave sounds like this:

Exercise 4   6/8 Cowbell pattern with hi-hat on quarter notes

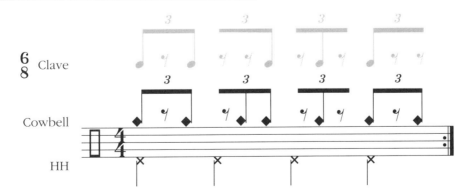

Playing quarter notes on the hi-hat helps lock in the bell pattern. Notice that this pattern is actually the clave figure with pickup notes before the third note and the first note of the clave pattern.

Again, the clave is *not* traditionally played in 6/8, we're only showing how the 6/8 clave relates to the 6/8 cowbell pattern.

Exercise 5 6/8 clave with pickup notes = 6/8 cowbell pattern

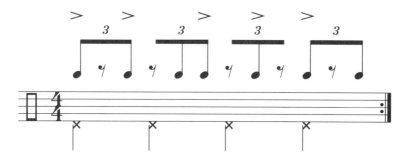

With the hi-hat playing quarter notes, try playing the cowbell figure with your right hand, while your left hand plays the clave pattern.

Exercise 6 6/8 cowbell pattern (right hand) with 6/8 clave (left hand)

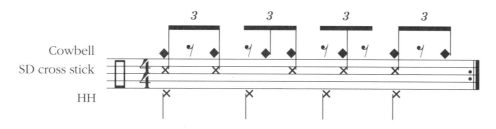

Adding the bass drum:

Now play the bass drum on beat 1, with an optional pickup on the last triplet note of "4."

Exercise 7 Bass drum figure 1 with 6/8 cowbell pattern

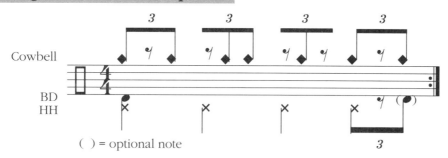

( ) = optional note

We can also play the bass drum with a kind of "2 feel." Play the bass drum on beats 1 and 3, with optional notes on the second triplet of "3" and the last triplet note of "4." The two optional notes give more of a swing, and a feeling of forward motion to the rhythm.

Exercise 8 Bass drum figure 2

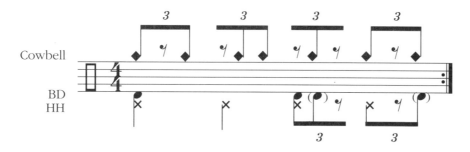

The toms on the drum set can imitate some of the basic conga parts that can be played to this Afro-Cuban 6/8 feel.

Exercise 9 Conga parts on toms

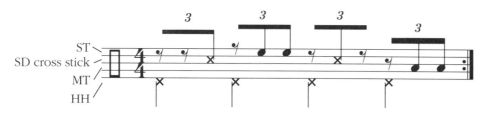

Let's put it all together.

AFRO-CUBAN 6/8 FEEL, FULL DRUMSET

Exercise 10 Afro-Cuban 6/8 feel (bembe) with full drumset

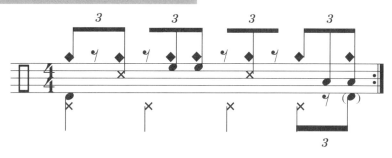

IDEAS:

The cowbell pattern can be played on the side of the floor tom for a wood sound, or played on the hi-hat imitating the shekere. If you play the cowbell pattern on the hi-hat, don't play quarter-notes on the hi-hat with your foot. Also try the cowbell pattern on the ride cymbal for a jazz or fusion feel.

Try leaving out the first note on the small tom. Now, the first note that you play on the tom falls on the clave pattern, making the rhythm more syncopated. At faster tempos this works well, it's less cluttered and swings harder.

Exercise 10a Leaving out the first note of the small tom

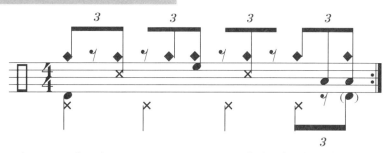

You can use bass drum figure 2 with optional pick up notes, to create a "2 feel," dividing the measure in half.

Exercise 10b Using bass drum figure 2

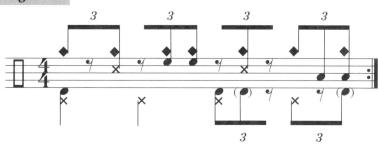

Opening the hi-hat with your foot on beat 1 of each measure will create a stronger feeling of downbeat, which is an important anchor for the 6/8 pattern.

Exercise 10c With hi-hat open on "1"

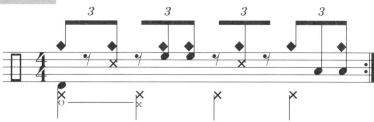

Let's hear the Afro-Cuban 6/8 feel played at a faster tempo. Listen to how the variations in bass drum and small tom parts change the feel. This 6/8 feel has a different "swing" to it at a faster tempo. Once you've learned the basic pattern, try it at different tempos and notice the differences.

Exercise 11 Faster Afro-Cuban 6/8 feel with full drum set and variations

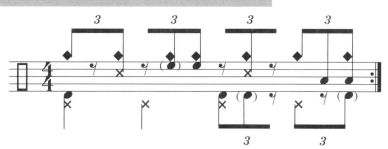

POLYRHYTHMIC 6/8 PATTERN, ABAKWA PATTERN

A *polyrhythm* is created when one rhythm is played over another. As you may have noticed, many polyrhythms are being played simultaneously in the Afro-Cuban 6/8 feel; different groupings are being played at the same time, against or over each other.

An important polyrhythm, "4 over 3," is also played in a different Afro-Cuban 6/8 feel than bembe. This is played traditionally by the *Abakwa,* a secret male society in Cuba. This rhythm is usually played with sticks on a wooden surface or on the side of a drum, or incorporated into one of the conga parts. The 6/8 cowbell pattern played in the bembe feel is *not* played with this pattern. The pattern looks and sounds like this:

Exercise 12   Polyrhythmic figure - Abakwa pattern

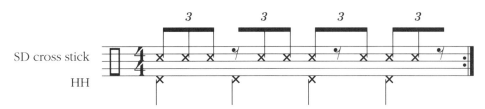

Notice that these are groupings of three triplet notes with a triplet rest, adding up to a grouping of four, played over the underlying triplet rhythm (groupings of three), creating the polyrhythm 4 over 3.

Exercise 12a

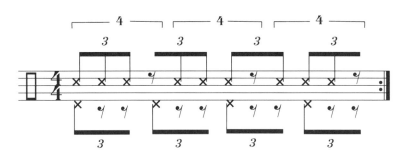

A full drumset adaptation sounds like this:

Exercise 13   Full drumset polyrhythmic figure - Abakwa pattern

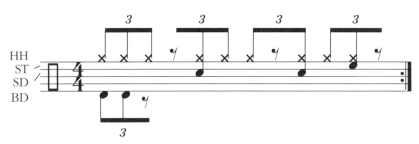

This polyrhythm can be played against the basic Afro-Cuban 6/8 feel, with a percussionist or another drumset player playing bembe, although this is *not* done traditionally with this pattern. This polyrhythm is also heard in the soloing played over different 6/8 feels, including bembe. It can also be heard in the jazz playing of Art Blakey, Elvin Jones and many others, reaching back to the West African 6/8 feel.

SOLOING

In traditional settings in West Africa and Cuba, a soloist will play over the 6/8 rhythm. In West Africa, a "master drummer" will lead the ensemble, "calling" the rhythms, telling when to start and stop, which rhythms to play and at what tempos, etc. He will also solo over the rhythm. Since this music is traditionally played to accompany dancing in both secular and religious settings, the master drummer's soloing will correspond to the improvisations of different solo dancers which is an important tradition in West African music. If you listen to various recordings from West Africa and Cuba, you will notice that the phrases used in soloing vary with different regions and people, but share a common approach.

Soloing is really "speaking" as if one were telling a story. Listen to the soloing played on the example of the Afro-Cuban 6/8 folkloric feel from Section 1 of the audio tape. Notice how it sometimes follows the clave and other times plays against the clave (creating polyrhythms). Notice also how some of the solo phrases stretch and play with the time, and that many of them end with a strong "1," in the style of the Afro-Cuban and West African 6/8 feels.

Soloing should be the last thing you attempt in learning the 6/8 rhythm. Traditionally in West Africa, a young boy starts on the cowbell, progresses to simple conga parts, then to more complicated conga parts. When he is fully versed in the rhythm, he may then be given an opportunity to play solo drum.

AFRO-CUBAN 6/8 PATTERNS WITH BACKBEATS

If we put a snare drum backbeat on beat 3, we have a half-time feel similar to that played in fusion music, the style that mixes jazz, R&B, funk, and Latin. Playing the 6/8 cowbell figure on the hi-hat takes the rhythm away from a more Afro-Cuban and West African sound and closer to a fusion or funk style. This feel is also heard in African popular music. The 6/8 pattern can also be played on the cowbell or ride cymbal for different textures and feels.

Different patterns with backbeat on "3"

Exercise 14 Afro-Cuban 6/8 feel with backbeat on "3"

Pattern 1, Snare drum on "3" and "4"

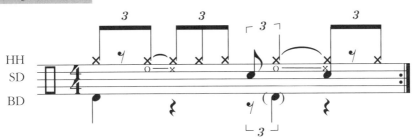

Pattern 2, Snare drum on "3"

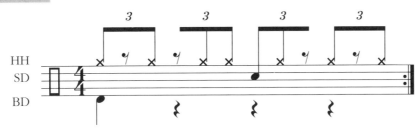

Pattern 3, Ride cymbal with hi-hat on "3" (No audio cue)

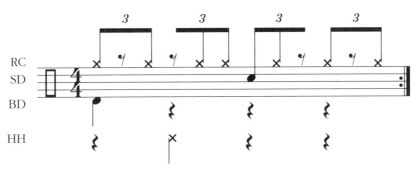

IDEAS:
Hi-Hat Patterns With the Foot
Playing different hi-hat patterns with your foot can create different feelings of time, as in Pattern 3, with the hi-hat just on beat 2. Other possibilities would be playing the hi-hat on beats 1 and 3 to emphasize the downbeats, or playing on the last triplet note of each beat, for an added push to the rhythm.

Bass Drum Patterns
If you play your bass drum with the clave or bell pattern, it will stay closer to the Afro-Cuban 6/8 feel. Playing quarter notes with less syncopation will bring it closer to funk and pop styles.

In the following exercises the hi-hat pattern can be played two different ways:
(1) The right hand plays the bell pattern, while the left hand plays the unaccented notes and snare drum backbeat.

(2) Playing hand to hand with the bell pattern accented by whichever hand the pattern falls on. In this example the right hand plays the snare drum backbeat.

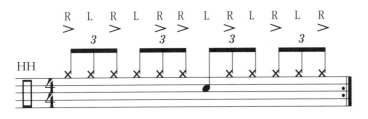

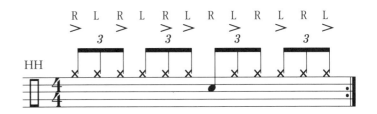

The second way is popular in the African pop feels because of the even, constant feel on the hi-hat.

Let's try some different bass drum variations:

Exercise 14a Bass drum Variation 1

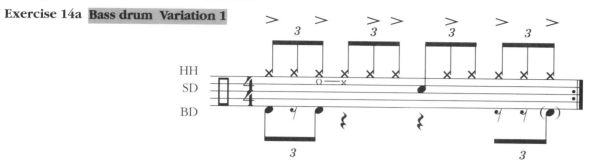

Opening the hi-hat on the last triplet note of "1" gives more drive to the rhythm. Try this alternating pattern:

Variation 2

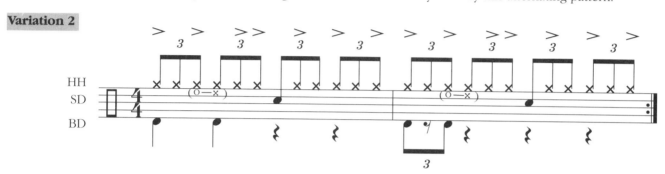

Notice the difference in syncopation versus straight quarter-notes. You can still open the hi-hat on the last triplet note of "1" over the straighter bass drum figure. Try it without opening the hi-hat at all for a different feel. Try leaving the bass drum off the first beat of the second measure.

Variation 3

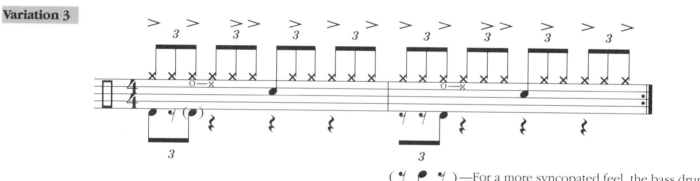

—For a more syncopated feel, the bass drum and hi-hat (open) play an eighth-note earlier.

Here's another two-bar pattern:

Variation 4

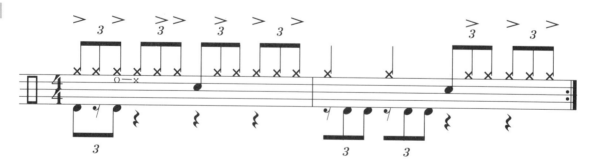

Now try the bass drum on all quarter notes. This is heard in popular music throughout Eastern, Southern and Central Africa.

Variation 5

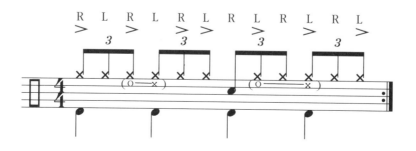

14

Now try backbeats on "2" and "4."

Exercise 15 `Afro-Cuban 6/8 feel with backbeats on "2" and "4"`

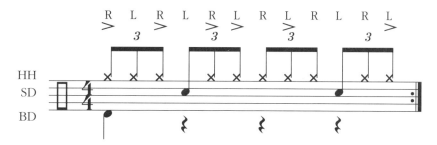

Bass drum variations with backbeats on "2" and "4."

EXERCISE 15a `Bass drum variations`

Variation 1

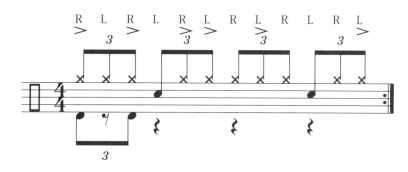

Variation 2

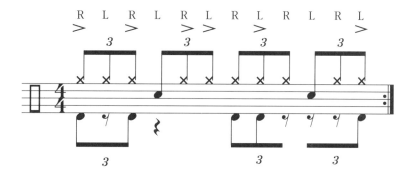

Variation 3

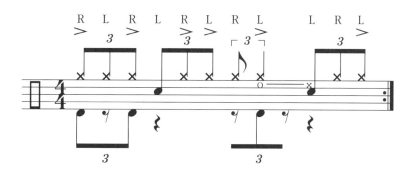

Variation 4 is typical of pop music from Central, Eastern and Southern Africa, where the bass drum often plays quarter notes with different hi-hat and snare drum parts. West African pop music tends to use more syncopated drum parts.

Variation 4

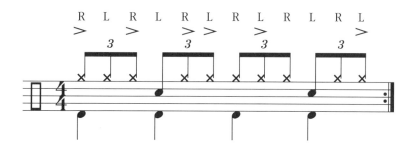

Hi-hat variations

The hi-hat can be opened for a more syncopated feel.

Exercise 15b `Hi-hat variation`

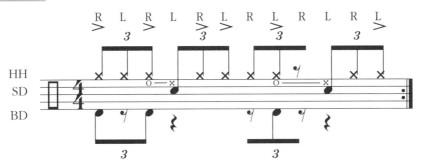

IDEAS:

The hi-hat pattern could be played on the ride cymbal during instrumental solos or louder musical sections. There's plenty of room for experimentation in blending the Afro-Cuban 6/8 feel with backbeats. Try playing the first backbeat on the last triplet note of "1" for an interesting syncopated feel.

AFRO-CUBAN 6/8 FEEL IN A JAZZ SETTING

The jazz feel, an American rhythm with West African roots, is also based on triplets.

Exercise 16 `Basic jazz feel (4/4)`

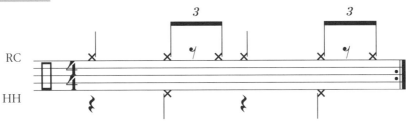

Try playing 2 bars of 4/4 jazz feel, then 2 bars of Afro-Cuban 6/8 feel. Play both feels on the ride cymbal, with the hi-hat on beats 2 and 4.

Exercise 17 `Two bars of jazz feel, to two bars of Afro-Cuban 6/8 feel`

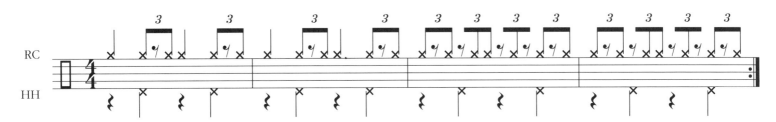

Notice that the jazz pattern has more of an *upbeat* feeling, emphasizing beats 2 and 4, while the 6/8 pattern has more of a downbeat feel, emphasizing beats 1 and 3. Some jazz standards, like "Invitation," have come to be played with an Afro-Cuban 6/8 feel in the "A" section, while the "B" section "swings" in a jazz feel. Try to listen to recordings and performances where these feels are played together. Many variations are played on the 6/8 feel. Try to hear the relationship between and common origin of the Afro-Cuban 6/8 and jazz ride pattern.

Two important pulses in a 3/4 jazz feel sound like this:

Exercise 18 `3/4 Jazz feel, two different pulses, two bars of each`

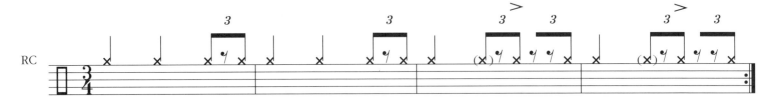

3/4 jazz feel, Elvin Jones-type pattern

This next example mixes a West African 6/8 feel with a 3/4 rolling triplet jazz feel. The toms are used in a way similar to the Afro-Cuban 6/8 pattern.

Exercise 19 3/4 Elvin Jones type pattern

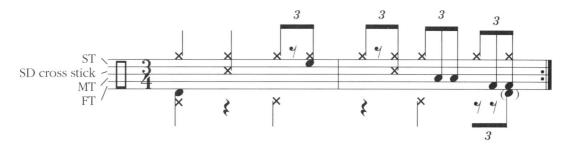

This example shows how the 6/8 cowbell figure can be stretched out and "swung" over a new triplet setting. Playing on just the last note of the triplets pushes the rhythm forward.

Exercise 19a Skeleton figure of Elvin Jones pattern

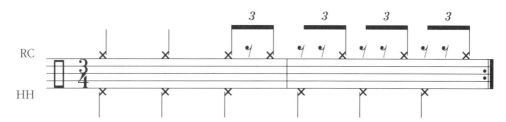

A few jazz tunes have been written using the Afro-Cuban 6/8 feel, the most famous being Mongo Santamaria's "Afro-Blue," which has been recorded by himself, John Coltrane (in a 3/4 jazz feel), and many others. It is a great vehicle for jazz improvisation over the Afro-Cuban 6/8 feel. Other tunes can be adapted to the 6/8 feel; listen to different possibilities.

SUMMARY

It has been said that all African and African-derived rhythms are actually in 6/8 time. What this means is that the 6/8 feel underlies the African-derived rhythms of Cuba, Brazil, the Caribbean, and the United States. Listen for phrases that sound like they're in 6/8. Remember that in African and Afro-Cuban music the distinction is not sharply made between 6/8 and 4/4, as in Western (i.e., Western European) music. African and Afro-Cuban rhythms are based on repeating phrases and figures and not on time signatures. We are using time signatures to adapt these rhythms to a form we are more familiar with.

SECTION 2
CLAVE IN 4/4 TIME

This clave in 4/4 is essentially the same pattern as the clave in 6/8, but phrased differently.

For review here's the 6/8 clave figure counted in 6/8 time:

Exercise 1 6/8 clave counted in 6/8 time

Played over triplets in 4/4 time it looks and sounds like this:

Exercise 2 6/8 clave counted in 4/4 time with triplets

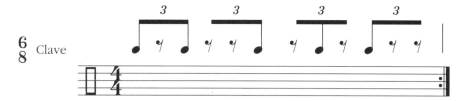

By changing the phrasing this same clave can be played in 4/4 time, using quarter and eighth-notes.

Exercise 3 Clave figure in 4/4 time

Although Exercise 3 is written with eighth-notes and quarter-notes, there is no actual difference in the length or time value of the notes. It actually sounds more like this:

Although you will usually see this clave written in eighth-notes, you could also write it with sixteenth-notes.

Clave

Try alternating two bars of clave in 6/8 with two bars of clave in 4/4. This exercise will help show the direct relationship between the two phrases. You can play 4, 8 or 16 bars of each phrase, playing clave with a snare drum cross stick and hi-hat on quarter notes.

Exercise 4 Two bars of 6/8 clave, to two bars of clave in 4/4

Clave

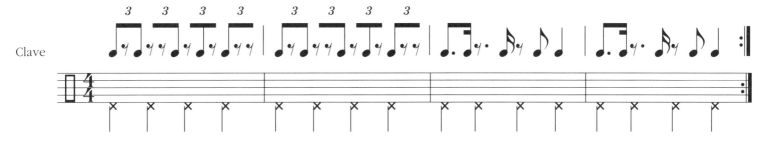

RUMBA CLAVE

This clave is called rumba clave because it is used in musical gatherings called *rumbas*. Rumbas are informal "get-togethers" combining African drumming and Spanish or African vocal traditions with improvised dancing and singing. **Rumba** also refers to the rhythms played at these gatherings. Although the rumba clave is counted in 4/4, it has a 6/8 feeling. Try to hear the 6/8 clave while you're playing in 4/4. This is the key to understanding rumba clave.

3-2, 2-3 clave

Looking at the two bar clave pattern in Exercise 5 you will notice that there are three notes in the first bar and two notes in the second bar. This is called *3-2 clave*. The first bar is called the *3-part* of the clave and the second bar is called the *2-part* of the clave. The *2-3 clave* is simply the reverse, starting with the 2 part of the clave.

Exercise 5 3-2 Rumba Clave

3–2 Rumba Clave

IDEAS:

As you have probably realized, once you're playing 3-2 or 2-3 clave, they sound alike. The only difference is where you call "1." Try playing 3-2 clave and without stopping, start counting 2-3 clave. By saying "1," you can mark where the phrase begins.

This exercise will strengthen your internal feel of clave. Most Afro-Cuban music goes in and out of 3-2 and 2-3 clave—it's knowing where you are *in* the clave pattern that is important.

Rumba clave is sometimes called *Cuban clave* because of its use in Cuban folkloric music. It is also sometimes called the *black clave*.

Exercise 6 2-3 Rumba Clave

2–3 Rumba Clave

SON CLAVE

Son is indigenous Cuban music combining African rhythms and Spanish harmonies. The *son* style laid the foundation for the popular Afro-Cuban dance music which emerged in Cuba, Puerto Rico, and New York City. The son clave is named for its use in son music. This clave is the same as a very popular and prevalent clave found throughout sub-Saharan Africa. It differs from the rumba clave by only one note, which gives it an entirely different feel. The son clave has a much stronger feel of 4/4 while the rumba clave retains a stronger 6/8 feel.

Let's listen to an example of 3-2 son clave.

Exercise 7 Son Clave 3-2

Frank Malabe

Now try two phrases of rumba clave followed by two phrases of son clave.

Exercise 8 **Four bars of 3-2 rumba clave to four bars of 3-2 son clave**

The son clave is sometimes called the *salsa clave* because of its use in **salsa,** the nickname for the Afro-Cuban dance music developed by the Puerto Rican community in New York City.

Exercise 9 3-2 Son Clave

Now the 2-3 son clave.

Exercise 10 2-3 Son Clave

20

ONE-BAR CLAVE

One of the most popular claves in the world is a *one bar* clave pattern. This clave is found in Africa, the Middle East, South America, Europe, the Caribbean, and the United States. We'll look at the African (and Spanish) uses of this clave, since they are the components of Afro-Cuban music.

An important drum played in the folkloric music called *conga* (Section 6) is the *bombo drum*. The bombo drum plays a one-bar clave figure. It muffles all notes except the second note of the rumba clave, which is played open and accented. Try playing the bombo pattern on your floor tom.

Exercise 11 Bombo drum pattern

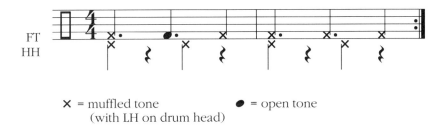

✗ = muffled tone
(with LH on drum head)   ● = open tone

The basic part played by the upright or electric bass in Afro-Cuban music comes from the one-bar clave figure. It is usually played with a silent "1." Here is the same rhythm played on the bass drum.

Exercise 12 Bass part played on bass drum

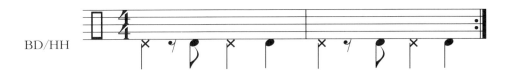

Harbor Performing Arts Center

SECTION 3
PALITO PATTERNS AND CASCARA

PALITO PATTERNS

For rumba, different stick patterns are played along with the clave. The sticks used are called palitos ("little sticks"). Traditionally, **palito** patterns are played on the **gua-gua**, which is a mounted piece of bamboo with a resonant hollow sound. We will be playing the palito patterns on the rim of the floor tom.

Most of the palito patterns are played with the rumba clave in the right hand and the rest of the pattern with your left hand. Let's start with the most popular palito pattern.

Exercise 1 Palito pattern, basic **(In Ex. 1-13, the quarter note count-off should be counted as half notes.)**

The clave figure within the palito pattern is *not* accented. The pattern should sound like one phrase with all notes at roughly the same volume. Think of the clave as you're playing and try to feel how the palito pattern falls on the clave. The clave is traditionally played by another person along with the palito patterns.

Sometimes a near-flam is played between beat 3 of the second measure and the "and" of beat 3. Also, the pickup into the next phrase ("and" of beat 4) can be a little rushed, giving more

of an edge to the rhythm. The hi-hat is included on "1" of each measure only as a reference and is not traditionally played.

Exercise 2 is another palito pattern that is often used. In this pattern the unaccented notes are played as ghost notes. Notice that this pattern breaks on the 2-part of the clave, giving a reference as to where the clave falls. Listen to the phrasing and again try to imitate it.

Exercise 2 Palito pattern 2

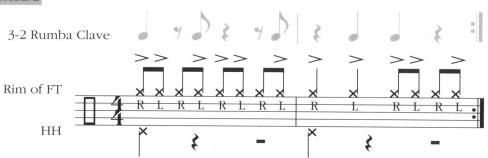

Our third palito pattern is also based on rumba clave. Remember, the clave within the palito pattern is *not* accented.

Exercise 3 Palito pattern 3

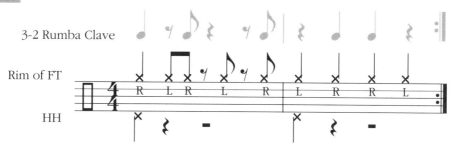

A fourth variation on the basic palito pattern differs from the first palito pattern in that the first note of the second measure is played on the "and" of "1."

Exercise 4 Palito pattern 4

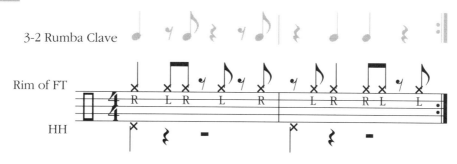

CASCARA

Cascara is the Spanish word for shell, referring to playing on the side or shell of the timbale. Cascara is played in salsa during verses and softer sections of music such as piano solos. On drum set we can imitate this technique on the side of the floor tom. The basic cascara pattern is the same as the basic palito pattern, except that it is played with one hand. The other hand (usually the left) plays a muffled tone on "2" and an open tone on "4" on the low timbale. Seeing timbales played live is the best way to understand how this works.

As son music moved from the rural areas to the cities the instrumentation changed. Bongos, maracas, and clave were played in early son bands. Arsenio Rodriguez, the great *tres* (a three-stringed guitar-like instrument) player and band leader, was one of the first to use congas in his ensembles. Eventually

timbales were added, creating a drum section of three drummers: a *conguero* playing congas, a *bongocero* playing bongos and handbell, and a *timbalero* playing timbales.

Timbale is the Spanish word for *timpani* (orchestral kettle drums). The timbales were the Cuban adaptation of the larger European drums which were used in *danzon orchestras.* The danzon orchestras played music for the upper classes, most of which was refined dance music from Europe and the United States (waltzes, foxtrots, *danzon,* etc.) From the danzon orchestras came *charangas,* which also played for upper class social gatherings. Timbales were used in charanga bands, and later congas were added. Timbales were eventually brought into the bands and orchestras playing son music, and have become an intregal part of the salsa rhythm section as well.

Let's try eight bars of the basic palito pattern with two hands to eight bars of the cascara pattern with one hand.

Exercise 5 Four bars of palito pattern (basic) with two hands, to four bars of cascara (right hand)

NOTE: Tape example says four bars of each but the actual number is eight.

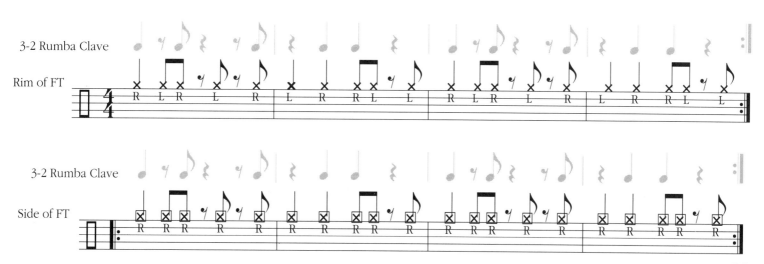

Cascara is not traditionally played to rumba clave but to son clave. We're playing it with rumba clave only to show how the cascara pattern is related to the rumba clave. Some of the modern bands in Cuba and New York City are using cascara with rumba clave.

Exercise 6 Cascara played with right hand (3-2 rumba clave)

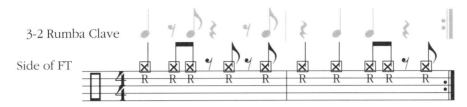

Try playing the cascara figure on the side of the floor tom while playing rumba clave with a cross stick on the snare drum. This is not a traditional pattern, but it is played by some current timbaleros, such as Nicky Marrero, and some modern bands in Cuba.

Exercise 7 Cascara in right hand, with 3-2 rumba clave in left hand

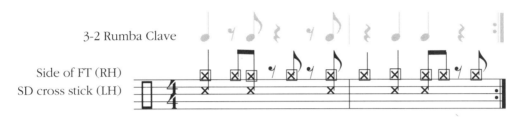

We can play the cascara figure 2-3 by reversing the measures of Exercise 7.

Exercise 8 Cascara in right hand (2-3 rumba clave)

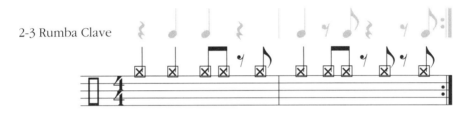

Now play 2-3 rumba clave with a snare drum cross stick while playing the 2-3 cascara pattern on the side of the floor tom.

Exercise 9 Cascara in right hand with 2-3 rumba clave in left hand

Let's see how cascara is traditionally played with son clave.

Exercise 10 Cascara in right hand with 3-2 son clave in left hand

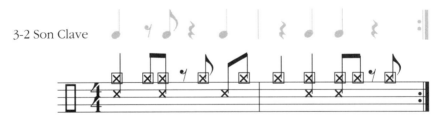

Now reverse the cascara pattern and try it with 2-3 son clave.

Exercise 11 Cascara in right hand with 2-3 son clave in left hand

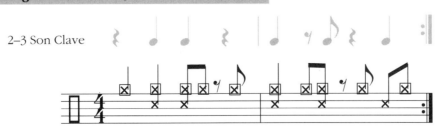

IDEAS:

Try the 3-2 cascara figure on the side of the floor tom and 3-2 son clave with a snare drum cross stick. After playing several 3-2 patterns without stopping, count "1" on the second bar of the pattern, changing it to a 2-3 pattern. After several 2-3 patterns go back to counting "1" at the beginning of the first bar. This is an important concept to learn because many charts for Afro-Cuban music will go in and out of 3-2 and 2-3 clave within the same song. All they are doing is starting figures and phrases on different parts of the *same* clave.

To help feel the difference between rumba and son clave, let's try four bars of cascara with rumba clave going to four bars of cascara with son clave.

Exercise 12 Four bars of cascara with 3-2 rumba clave to four bars of cascara with 3-2 son clave

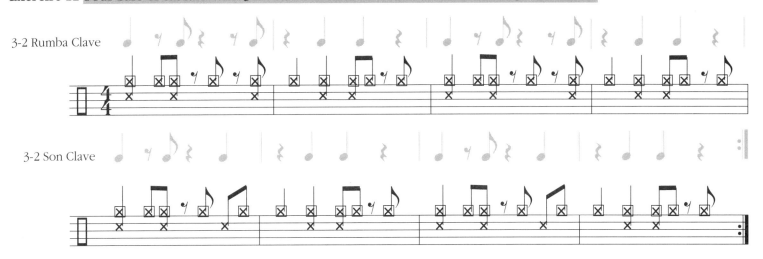

Let's try the same exercise played 2-3.

Exercise 13 Four bars of cascara (RH) with 2-3 rumba (LH) clave to four bars of cascara (RH) with 2-3 son clave (LH)

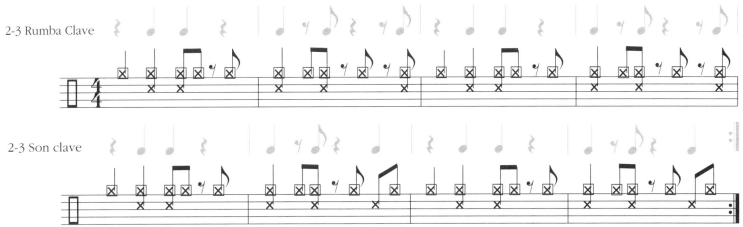

Let's listen to the basic conga drum pattern played in son music, called **tumbao.**

Exercise 14a Tumbao on congas played to 3-2 son clave

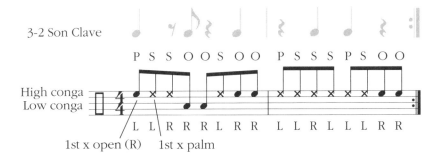

Exercise 14b Tumbao played to 2-3 son clave

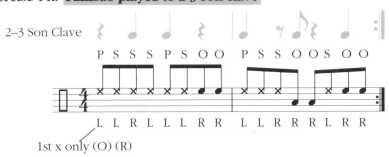

Until recently, Afro-Cuban dance music did not involve drumset. In adapting traditional rhythms played in son music to the drumset, we can look to the timbales.

Let's listen to timbales played with a conga player. Notice the metallic sound of the timbale shell. Timbale sticks are untapered, without tips and narrower than drum sticks. They are played with matched grip. The right hand plays cascara on the side of the timbale while the palm of the left hand plays muffled and open tones on the lower of the two timbales. This compliments the tumbao figure with a single note on "4" instead of two notes. The ruff and rim shot that opens the rhythm is called *abanico,* meaning "fan". Abanico is used to open and close sections of tunes and to set up figures. Abanico is used especially in 2-3 patterns. It can be played as a four-stroke ruff or five-stroke roll.

Exercise 15 On timbales, cascara with a conga player (3-2 son clave)

X = muffled tone ● = open tone

Exercise 16 On timbales, cascara played with a conga player (2-3 son clave)

BOMBO NOTE

The second note of 3-2 clave is called the bombo note because the **bombo drum** played in the *conga* rhythm accents this note of the clave. The bombo note is accented in folkloric music (congas, rumbas, etc.) as well as the popular dance music styles (son music, mambos, etc.). In the bombo drum pattern all notes are muffled except the bombo note.

Let's try the cascara pattern with the bombo note played with the bass drum.

Exercise 17 On drumset, cascara in right hand with a conga player (3-2 son clave)

(SD – snares off for timbale sound)

Exercise 18 On drumset, cascara in right hand with a conga player (2-3 son clave)

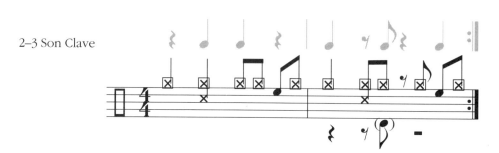

When playing without a conga player you can add an extra tom note on the "and" of "4" imitating the tumbao pattern.

Exercise 19 Cascara pattern without a conga player (3-2 son clave)

3–2 Son Clave

The bass drum can imitate the lower conga drum by playing two notes on the three part of the clave which answers the tumbao figure played on the higher conga.

Let's try the same pattern played to 2-3 son clave.

Exercise 20 Cascara pattern without a conga player (2-3 son clave)

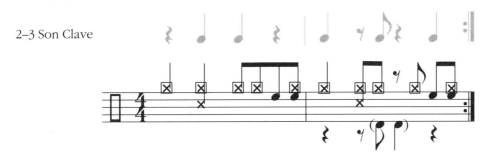

2–3 Son Clave

Here's a syncopated cascara variation which is played in Cuba. This pattern uses only certain notes of the basic cascara pattern. Some bands in Cuba, such as Los Van Van, use this cascara variation.

Exercise 21 Syncopated cascara variation (2-3 rumba clave)

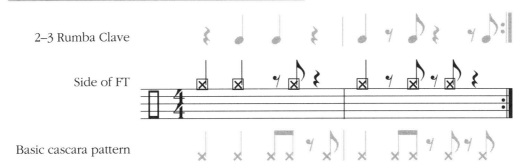

2–3 Rumba Clave

Side of FT

Basic cascara pattern

Use of the hi-hat

Since the hi-hat is not part of the timbale set-up, it is of course not usually heard in Afro-Cuban music. Playing the hi-hat also tends to interrupt the syncopated flow of the cascara patterns. However, as a great independence exercise you could try playing the clave pattern with your left foot on the hi-hat. In fact, you can try playing clave with the hi-hat in many of the different sections of this book.

But remember, the hi-hat is not a traditional sound in Afro-Cuban music–it is used more in African popular music, Calypso, Reggae, Brazilian music, jazz and rhythm and blues. The hi-hat can be played with the 6/8 feel, mozambique and songo, not in their traditional forms but more in the styles of funk and fusion.

Caribbean Cultural Center

The Tito Puente percussion section

SECTION 4
BELL PATTERNS

The timbale set-up includes a *mambo bell* which is a long, wide, low-pitched bell, and a *cha-cha bell* a small, high-pitched bell. The mambo bell is used in many of the dance feels based on son music, especially **mambo,** which was made popular in Cuba in the late 1930's. The cha-cha bell is used mostly in **cha-cha-cha**, which was a dance created by charanga orchestras in the 1950's.

MAMBO BELL PATTERNS

In softer sections of dance music (such as verses and piano solos), the cascara pattern is played on the side of the timbales. During louder sections (choruses and some instrumental solos), the mambo bell is played. We will hear how both patterns work in the popular dance music based on son which includes mambo, and the New York City style called *salsa*.

The mambo bell is mounted on the timbales so that it lies perpendicular (at a 90-degree angle) to the player. Played with timbale sticks, the stick strikes across the middle of the bell.

The most common mambo bell figure sounds like this:

Exercise 1 Mambo bell pattern (2-3) with son clave

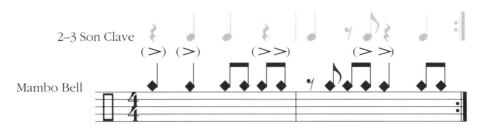

We have written the accented notes in parentheses because although the notes are accented it is important not to *over* accent them. We'll only write in the accents one time for the 2-3 and 3-2 patterns, but remember the accents are part of the mambo bell patterns.

The son clave is the clave heard most often with mambo bell patterns. Notice how the mambo bell pattern synchronizes with the 2-part of the clave. This can be helpful in finding the clave pattern. Let's play the 2-3 son clave with a snare drum cross stick.

Exercise 2 Mambo bell pattern with 2-3 son clave

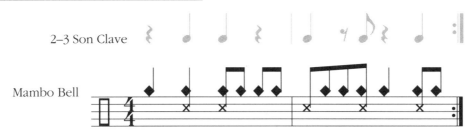

It's difficult to place a cowbell on the drumset at the same angle used in the timbale set-up. Most cowbells that are mounted on the bass drum have the mouth of the bell pointing towards you. This will work fine, just play the patterns on the middle part of the bell, preferably with the butt end of the stick for a fuller sound. Let's try the mambo bell pattern played 3-2.

Exercise 3 Mambo bell pattern 3-2 (3-2 son clave)

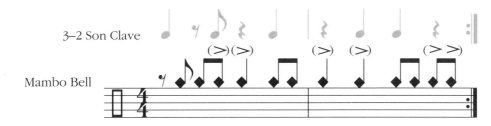

Now let's add the clave rhythm with the left hand. Notice the silent "1" in the bell part and how it relates to the clave.

Exercise 4 Mambo bell pattern, with 3-2 son clave

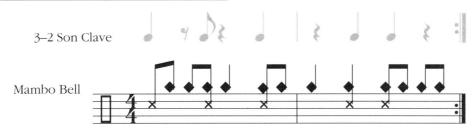

Returning to the 2-3 pattern, with the left hand play a snare drum cross stick on "2," and small tom on "4." The right hand plays the mambo bell pattern. This is what a timbalero would play, except that he would muffle beat 2 with the left hand instead of playing the rim.

Exercise 5 Mambo bell pattern 2-3, with a conga player

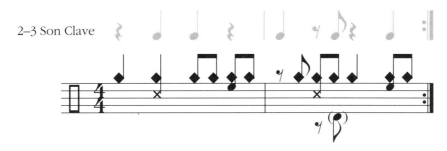

As we saw before, when playing cascara on drumset with a conga player (Section 3, #17), the bass drum can play the bombo note. Because this rhythm is derived from a timbale pattern, the hi-hat will not be used. Playing "2" and "4" on the hi-hat can sometimes work if you think of it as part of the guiro rhythm and not as backbeats. Again, listening to recordings and live performances will help you learn the right phrasing.

When playing without a conga player, you can play the conga part on the small tom. The bass drum can play the notes shown in the second measure imitating the lower conga part.

Let's try the mambo bell pattern (2-3) without a conga player.

Exercise 6 Mambo bell pattern (2-3) without a conga player

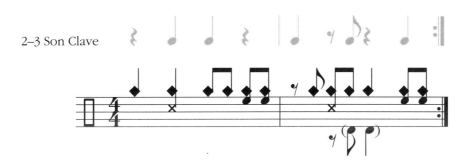

Now we will hear the same patterns played to 3-2 clave.

Exercise 7 `Mambo bell pattern (3-2) with a conga player`

If there is no conga player, you can play the conga part on the small tom.

Exercise 8 `Mambo bell pattern (3-2) without a conga player`

Here are some other mambo bell patterns that can be played as variations for mambo and related dance feels. These patterns were written out by Johnny Armendra, who teaches timbales at the Boy's Harbor School in East Harlem and has played with many great salsa bands. At time of publication he is playing with Mongo Santamaria. These patterns can be played 3-2 or 2-3. Many of these patterns work well for conga, bongo, or instrumental solos.

Exercise 9 `Mambo bell variations played to 3-2 son clave` (with one clave phrase between each)

BONGO BELL PATTERNS

As well as playing bongos, the bongocero plays a cowbell called *campana* or **bongo bell**. This cowbell has a wider, thicker bell with a "fatter," lower sound. Played with a short, round piece of wood, the mouth and middle of the bell are played, producing two different sounds. The bongo bell is played in certain sec-

tions of son style dance music, along with the mambo bell. The bongo bell pattern adds drive to the rhythm and plays an important role in emphasizing the downbeat (played on the mouth of the bell). The basic bongo bell pattern is as follows.

Exercise 10 Hand-held bongo bell pattern (2-3 son clave)

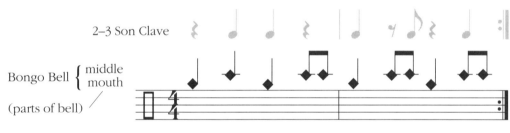

Notice that on the 2-part of the clave only one note is played on the middle of the bell. This is your key to where the 2-part of the clave falls. This pattern can be played 3-2 by reversing the figure.

Exercise 11 Hand-held bongo bell pattern, played to 3-2 son clave

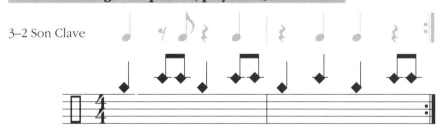

Now we will play the bongo bell pattern on a mounted bell with the right hand and add the son clave with snare drum cross stick. We will use both 2-3 and 3-2 son clave.

Exercise 12 Bongo bell pattern played with right hand on mounted cowbell, with 2-3 son clave in left hand

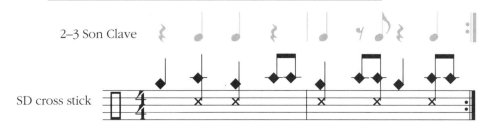

Exercise 13 Bongo bell pattern played with right hand on mounted cowbell, with 3-2 son clave in the left hand

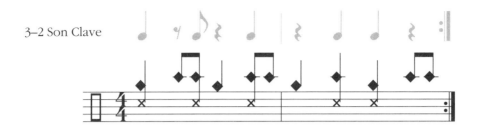

3–2 Son Clave

Bongo bell patterns with a conga player

You can play this pattern with the basic left hand timbale pattern that we used before with cascara and the mambo bell pattern.

Exercise 14 Bongo bell pattern with a conga player (2-3 son clave)

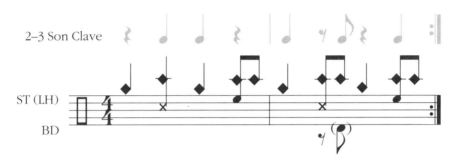

2–3 Son Clave

ST (LH)

BD

Exercise 15 Bongo bell pattern with a conga player (3-2 son clave)

3–2 Son Clave

Exercise 16 Bongo bell pattern without a conga player (2-3 son clave)

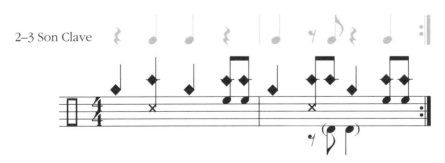

2–3 Son Clave

Exercise 17 Bongo bell pattern without a conga player (3-2 son clave)

3–2 Son Clave

Here is a popular bongo bell variation that can be used.

Exercise 18 Bongo bell variation (2-3 son clave)

This pattern or the cascara pattern (on the middle part of the bell) are often played during timbale or conga solos.

MAMBO BELL AND BONGO BELL PATTERNS TOGETHER

Here's what the two bell patterns sound like played together. Notice where the patterns overlap and how they both fall on the clave. Listen for the 2-part of the clave where both patterns meet with the clave.

Exercise 19 Mambo bell and bongo bell played together, two bells (2-3 son clave)

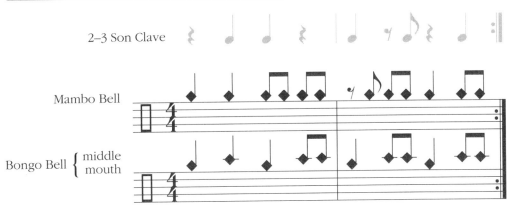

IDEAS:

You can try playing both patterns on two bells to build independence. The higher-pitched, thinner-sounding bell can play the mambo bell pattern while the lower-pitched, fatter-sounding bell plays the bongo bell pattern. The great percussionist Changuito of the Cuban band Los Van Van plays both mambo bell and bongo bell parts (on two bells) in his timbale set-up. You can try playing both bell parts on one bell.

Certain cowbells, like the LP© Timbale Bell, have a wide mouth and a clear high-pitched body which allows you to play a combination of the two parts. On a mambo or bongo bell, playing both parts doesn't sound right. The mouth of the mambo bell is too thin and the body of the bongo bell is too low-sounding.

Here's a pattern which includes both mambo and bongo bell parts.

Exercise 20 Mambo and bongo bell patterns played together with one hand on mounted cowbell on bass drum (2-3 son clave)

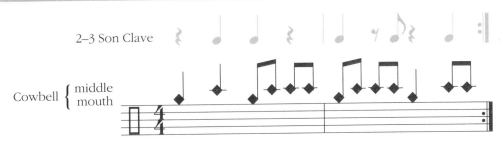

This is basically what one hears when both bells are played. This combination can get "busy" and works better at slower tempos.

CHA-CHA BELL

The ***Cha-cha-cha*** was a dance created by the charanga orchestras in Cuba in the early 1950's. Charanga orchestras were groups which played for the upper classes in Cuba, using piano, violins, flute, upright bass and timbales. These orchestras played European dance music and refined styles of Cuban dance music. The sound was less rhythmic than son music, which was more syncopated due to the influence of African rhythms. Congas were added later to charanga orchestras. Son orchestras also played the cha-cha feel using congas.

Let's listen to the basic cha-cha feel. It is a straight quarter-note feel which is *not* played to clave. This is why it doesn't swing like the cascara or mambo bell patterns, which *are* syncopated and played to clave. You may sometimes see clave played to a cha-cha feel. It may be played by a singer who is used to playing clave on other dance feels, but this is not traditionally done. Remember, the cha-cha pattern doesn't "fall" on either side of the clave.

The instruments that you hear will be conga playing tumbao, cha-cha bell and small tom playing the timbale part, and guiro.

Exercise 21 Basic cha-cha feel

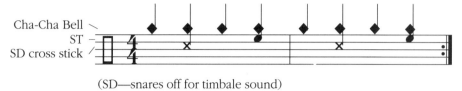

Cha-Cha Bell
ST
SD cross stick

(SD—snares off for timbale sound)

Here is the guiro rhythm usually played for cha-cha.

Exercise 22 Guiro

Guiro

= scraping with no specific rhythmic subdivision of notes

Exercise 23 Hi-hat playing the guiro figure

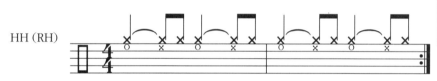

HH (RH)

This rhythm can be played on the hi-hat with either hand or the foot at slower tempos. You can play the basic cha-cha bell pattern (quarter-notes) with the right hand and the hi-hat guiro part with the left hand. Another possibility is reversing the hands: playing the cha-cha bell with the left hand and the right hand playing the hi-hat. In the next example, the hi-hat is playing part of the guiro rhythm with the foot. Notice that the eighth-notes after beats 2 and 4 are not played.

Let's listen to the cha-cha feel played on drumset with a conga player.

Exercise 24 Cha-cha feel with a conga player

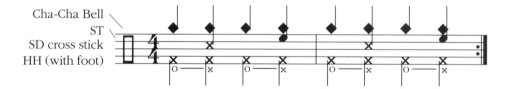

Cha-Cha Bell
ST
SD cross stick
HH (with foot)

The cha-cha bell pattern can be played on ride cymbal for more of a jazz feel. This was done by Mongo Santamaria with tunes such as "Watermelon Man." The ride cymbal figure can be played as straight quarter-notes or eighth-notes accenting the downbeats.

Exercise 25 Cha-cha feel without a conga player

BD

Caribbean Cultural Center

Dancer /Percussionist Papaito

SECTION 5
GUAGUANCO

RUMBA

Rumba is a form of folkloric drumming, singing and dancing which uses African rhythms, mostly Spanish vocal refrains, and African dance improvisations. The three most popular forms of rumba are **guaguanco**, **yambu,** and **columbia.** *Rumba columbia* is played with a 6/8 feel and sung in a combination of Spanish and African phrases. *Rumba yambu* is traditionally played on different-sized boxes which have been hollowed out (called **cajones**), and is sung in Spanish. *Rumba guaguanco* is the most popular rumba, especially in Puerto Rico and New York City. Guaguanco is played by a group that consists of three drummers, using congas of different sizes and tones. The three drums used are the **quinto** (the solo drum), **Salidor** (the time-keeper), and **tres golpes** (the accompaniment).

Quinto is the name of the high drum which solos over the rhythm and vocal vamps. Traditionally, the quinto is played to accompany dancers. The vocals are often improvised commentaries on people, the news, etc. The traditional instruments for guaguanco include clave, palito, and congas. Rumba clave is usually played for guaguanco.

Let's listen to an example of guaguanco played with clave, palito pattern, two congas and quinto drum. The low drum is called *salidor* and the second or higher part is the *tres golpes* (literally meaning "three blows" in Spanish). You will hear everything together, then each part separately so that you can see how it all fits together.

(Start of side two of tape)
GUAGUANCO, FOLKLORIC FEEL

3-2 Rumba clave

Palito pattern basic

Low drum (salidor) played by one drummer, holding down the rhythm.

Middle drum (tres golpes) answers the low drum (variations can be used)

35

The quinto solos over the rhythm. Here is the quinto solo written out.

Transcription by John Riley

3-2 Rumba Clave

Guaguanco pattern enters on tape.

Guaguanco on congas

Here's the guaguanco figure which we just heard with two players, played by one conga player, as it would be in non-folkloric situations.

Exercise 1 Guaguanco figure on conga (3-2 rumba clave)

Basic conga melody

GUAGUANCO ON DRUMSET

Let's adapt this to the drumset. We can play the floor tom and small tom imitating the conga "melody," or substitute other toms depending on the tuning of your drums. The figures played around the basic guaguanco pattern are adaptations of the conga parts.

Exercise 2 Guaguanco figure on drums

The guaguanco figure we've been using is the most popular and well-known guaguanco figure. There are many other possibilities and variations.

Exercise 3 Guaguanco figure on toms (four variations four bars of each)

Basic guaguanco figure

Variation 1

Variation 2

Variation 3

Variation 4

Variations 1-4 with all parts written in

Notice how the accented snare drum notes "answer" the guaguanco figure.

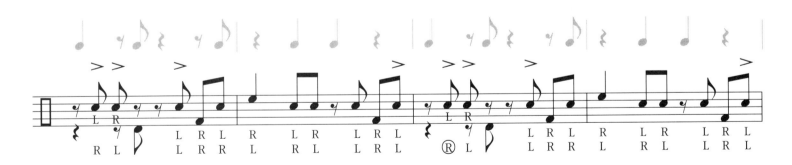

Try playing clave with the right hand on the side of the floor tom while playing the basic guaguanco figure on the toms with the left hand.

Exercise 4 Playing clave with the right hand on the side of the floor tom, guaguanco figure with the left hand on toms

(Bombo note)

You can try reversing the hands, playing clave with the left hand (snare drum cross stick) and the guaguanco figure on the toms with the right hand. This will help you feel where the guaguanco figure falls on the clave. Notice that the "active" part of the clave (the high tom part) falls on the 2-part of the clave. This is called "playing against the clave" because the figure doesn't synchronize with the clave, but seems to go against it. One of the hardest parts of learning guaguanco is learning to feel it against the clave. This takes time so don't get discouraged. After plenty of listening and practicing this won't feel or sound so strange.

Exercise 4a (same as exercise 4, with reversed hands)

(Bombo note)

Now let's try the palito pattern on the side of the floor tom and the guaguanco figure on toms.

Exercise 5 Palito pattern (RH) on side of floor tom, guaguanco figure on toms

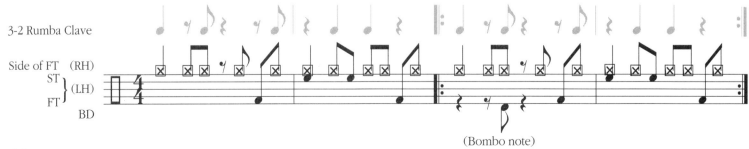

(Bombo note)

The palito pattern can be played on the bell of the ride cymbal for a different texture while the bass drum answers the guaguanco figure played on the toms. This can be used in jazz and fusion settings.

Exercise 6 Guaguanco figure on full drumset without a conga player (3-2 rumba clave)

You can try leaving out beat 1 in the bass drum part and just play the bombo note, making the rhythm more syncopated. The bombo note is an important accent played in the conga part, so be sure to accent it on the bass drum.

When playing guaguanco with a conga player, the conga player will play the guaguanco figure against the clave and the drumset player can answer, playing the figure with the clave.

Exercise 7 Guaguanco, full drumset with a conga player

Set-up figures for bombo note with variations

In the guaguanco rhythm, the bombo note is "set up" by playing different figures. These figures are usually played on the solo (quinto) drum. We'll play them with accents on the snare drum.

Exercise 8 Set-up figures for bombo note

41

GUAGUANCO VARIATIONS FOR DRUMSET

Exercise 9 **Different variations that can be played on drumset, for guaguanco**

3-2 Rumba Clave

Caribbean Cultural Center

SECTION 6
CONGA

One of the most exciting times in Cuba is Carnival (Spanish, *Carnaval*). Celebrated during the week before Lent, Carnival was originally a European Christian festival. Today in Trinidad, Brazil, Haiti, Cuba and many other Caribbean and South American countries, Carnival has become a week-long celebration complete with continuous music, dancing, singing and costumes.

Conga refers to the musical rhythm as well as the dance that takes place in the streets of Cuba during Carnival time. The Carnival parade itself is called *comparsa*. In the comparsa, large ensembles of drummers, brass players, dancers and singers take to the streets for a frenzied celebration.

CONGA, FOLKLORIC FEEL

Let's listen to conga (the rhythm) as it is played traditionally in the comparsa. Conga is danced with a step backward on the bombo note. Notice how the rhythm falls on the clave (rumba clave) and how the bombo note is accented by the bombo drum. After we hear the rhythm, we'll isolate the different parts.

Note: In this case the *high drum* is called the salidor.

High drum (salidor)

Middle drum (rebajador)

M = muffled

Low drum (conga)

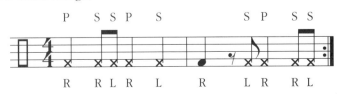

Section 6, Conga (folkloric feel)

Clave on handbell

Bombo drum

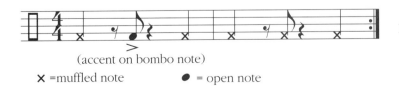

(accent on bombo note)

✕ =muffled note   ● = open note

43

Snare drum

Secondary bell 3

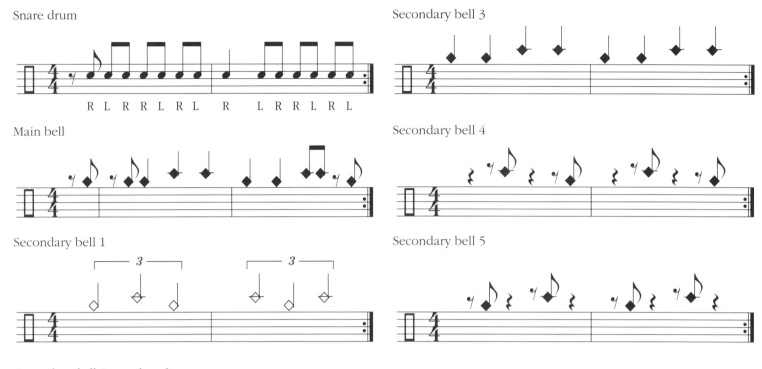

Main bell

Secondary bell 4

Secondary bell 1

Secondary bell 5

Secondary bell 2 not played on tape.

CONGA, SNARE, AND BASS DRUM PATTERNS

Let's try the snare drum pattern. We'll play the following patterns with 2-3 rumba clave. Check the tape to help with phrasing.

Exercise 1 Basic snare drum pattern played to 2-3 rumba clave

Now let's try the bombo drum pattern on the bass drum, accenting the bombo note.

Exercise 2 Bombo drum pattern on bass drum

Next we will add the bombo drum pattern to the snare drum pattern. The snare drum and bombo drum parts should feel and sound like one part.

Exercise 3 Snare drum and bombo pattern on bass drum, together

CONGA, FULL DRUMSET

Here's a pattern for drumset that accents the bombo note on the floor tom.

Exercise 4 Basic conga pattern for drumset

Here are some variations that you can use. These are similar to the set-up figures for the bombo note we played in the section on guaguanco. Flams are optional. Try playing only one flam per measure.

Exercise 5 Variations on basic conga pattern for drumset

BELL PARTS FOR CONGA

Here is another basic bell part for conga which you can play on cowbell.

Exercise 6   Basic bell part for conga

Exercise 6a   Main bell part for conga, folkloric feel

Either of the two previous bell patterns will work fine as a basic or main bell part for conga.

SECTION 7
MOZAMBIQUE

Adapted from the conga rhythm, **mozambique** was made popular by Pello el Afrokan in Cuba, and later popularized in New York City by Eddie Palmieri (with Manny Oquendo on timbales). The rhythm has no specific relationship to the African nation of Mozambique, and the name was probably coined as a catch-word associating the music with Africa.

MOZAMBIQUE ON TIMBALES

The first example of mozambique is the basic mozambique timbale rhythm, played on drumset. Notice how the low timbale (or middle tom) plays part of the bombo drum rhythm. The cha-cha bell figure is similar to the snare drum part played for conga.

Exercise 1   Mozambique, basic timbale pattern

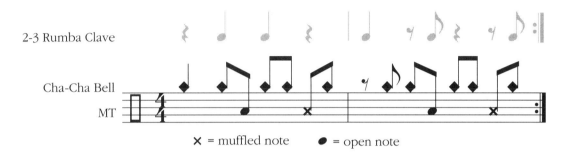

X = muffled note   ● = open note

MOZAMBIQUE ON DRUMSET

Let's try adapting the mozambique pattern to full drumset.

Exercise 2   Mozambique pattern on drumset

You can use different bass drum figures to set up the "and" of "4" on the snare drum.

Exercise 3   Bass drum variations for mozambique pattern on drumset (2-3 rumba clave)

Variation 1

2-3 Rumba Clave

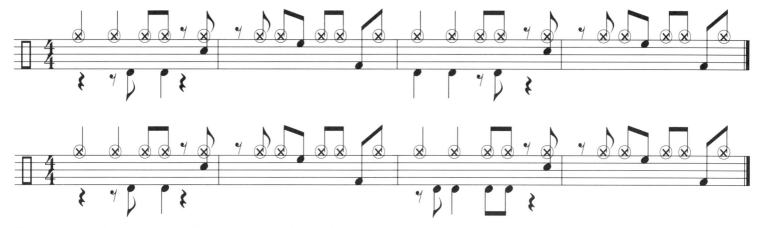

The next example is a variation that can be played with the mozambique pattern on drumset.

Exercise 4 **Variation on mozambique pattern on drum set**

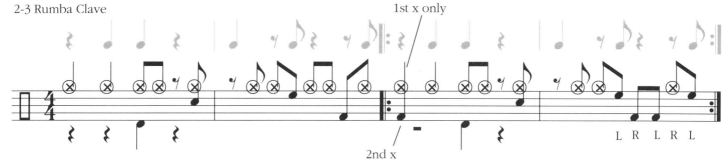

More variations on drumset.

Exercise 5 **More variations on mozambique pattern**

STEVE GADD MOZAMBIQUE PATTERN

Steve Gadd plays a mozambique variation in some of his soloing. Let's see what he uses as a basic pattern.

Exercise 6 **Steve Gadd mozambique pattern (basic)**

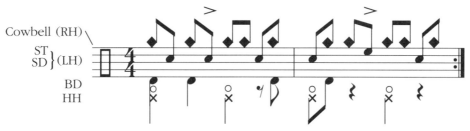

Here are a few variations to the basic mozambique pattern. The snare is played like a flam with the cowbell on beat 1.

Exercise 7 **Steve Gadd mozambique pattern with variations**

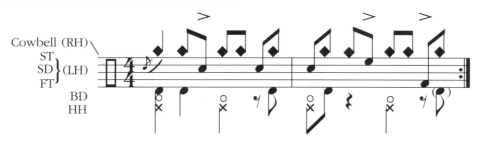

Steve Gadd plays another mozambique variation using four sticks on "Late In The Evening" by Paul Simon. For a demonstration, refer to "Steve Gadd - Up Close," an instructional video available from DCI Music Video.

MOZAMBIQUE PATTERN FOR TWO DRUMSETS

Next is a four-bar mozambique pattern for two drumsets. The first drumset plays upbeats and syncopations while the second drumset plays more of a steady 16th-note pattern on the hi-hat.

Exercise 8 **Four bar mozambique pattern for two drumsets**

First Drumset

Second Drumset

(Pattern starts in the 3rd bar)

Bob Weiner

SECTION 8
SONGO

Now we come to a rhythm actually created for the drumset! Attributed to the great percussionist Changuito of the Cuban group Los Van Van, songo was adapted to the music of the 70's and 80's.

Let's look at the basic pattern. Played with all rim sounds, it sounds like a 2-3 palito pattern. Notice how the songo pattern falls on the clave.

The bass drum plays the bombo drum accent in each measure. Notice that the bass drum plays the accent in both measures over both parts of the clave (like the bombo drum and the low timbale in mozambique). Remember that with cascara, mambo and bongo bell patterns, and guaguanco, the bombo note was accented only in the 3-part of the clave.

BASIC SONGO PATTERN

Exercise 1 Basic songo pattern with two hands played to 2-3 rumba clave

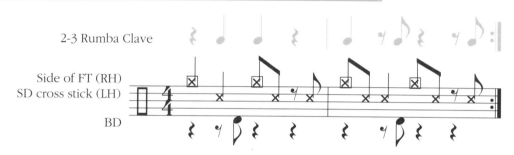

Exercise 2 Basic songo pattern with right hand playing cowbell and left hand playing snare drum rim

Notice how playing "1" and "3" on the cowbell changes the feel. This same contrast of downbeats and upbeats happens between the bongo bell (downbeats 1 and 3) and mambo bell (syncopated with lots of upbeats). The bass drum can play an optional note on "1," giving an added push to the rhythm, but if you play on "1" all the time it will interupt the flow of the rhythm.

Now let's move the left hand around to the different drums.

Exercise 3 Basic songo pattern on full drumset

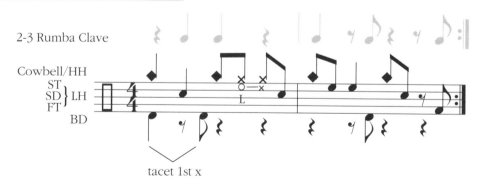

IDEAS:

With the right hand try playing hi-hat, ride cymbal or the side of the floor tom for different textures. In Cuba, different bells are played on each downbeat, creating an exciting feel with both hands constantly playing different sounds. The hi-hat (with the foot) can play on "1" and "3." Playing quarter notes tends to be too busy and playing on "2" and "4" clashes with the downbeat feel of the rhythm.

SONGO VARIATIONS

Here's a variation on the basic songo pattern. This variation, also played by Changuito, adds variety and breaks up the basic pattern. Notice how it falls on the clave. You'll hear the basic songo pattern played once so you can hear how to go to the variation.

Exercise 4 Basic songo pattern with variation

At faster tempos you can play fewer notes with the left hand. The bass drum plays on "1" in the first measure and does not play in the second measure.

Exercise 5 Songo pattern for faster tempos

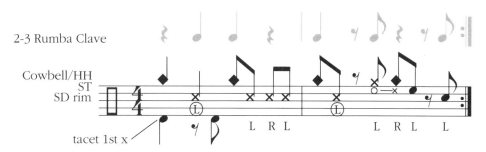

Here is a different songo pattern using the middle and floor tom. This pattern has a very different feel than the basic songo pattern. Notice that the middle tom is played with the right hand while the left hand plays "2" on the snare drum rim. The middle tom can be played on "2" *without* the snare drum rim (with the left hand), which will work better when playing faster tempos.

Exercise 6 Songo pattern 2

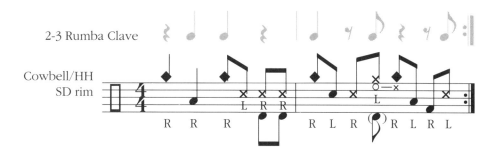

Now let's try playing the middle tom on the "and" of "2." This makes the feel more syncopated. This variation will be difficult at first because playing the middle tom between the cowbell notes breaks the even "1" and "3" feel in the right hand.

Exercise 7 Songo pattern 2 with syncopated middle tom figure in measure 1

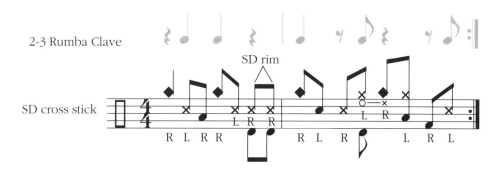

Here is a songo pattern not included on the tape, with a melodic pattern on the toms.

Songo pattern 3

Most songo patterns that we hear are played "2-3." Frank Malabe has come up with a "3-2" songo for two drumsets. The first pattern can be played by itself or the second drumset can be added if there are two drummers. Notice that you are playing "3-2" rumba clave with a snare drum cross stick which is answered by the small tom and bass drum. The last measure is actually the first measure of the basic "2-3" songo pattern.

Exercise 8 Mala-songo four bar pattern for two drumsets in 3-2 rumba clave

Drumset 1

Drumset 2

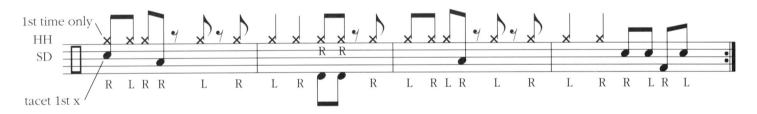

Songo is one of the most adaptable Afro-Cuban rhythms. Playing downbeats on the cowbell, hi-hat or ride cymbal makes this rhythm fit in with pop, funk and fusion styles. Some of the best examples of bands playing songo are the Cuban bands Los Van Van, Afro-Cuba, Ritmo Orientale and Irakere, and from Puerto Rico, Batacumbele and Zaperoko with Frankie Rodriguez.

Caribbean Cultural Center

Millie, Jocelyn, y los Vecinos

SECTION 9
MERENGUE

Even though it is not Afro-Cuban, *merengue* is an important rhythm with African roots. Merengue is a rhythm and dance from the Dominican Republic, the Spanish-speaking part of the island called Hispaniola. Haiti makes up the other part of the island and has wonderful folkloric and popular dance music, including its own version of merengue.

The basic merengue pattern traditionally has three parts or sections. The first section is called *merengue.* The second section (which most people call merengue) is called *jaleo.* The third section which is sometimes referred to as the "swing section" is called *apanpichao.*

A double-headed drum, the *tambora,* plays an important role in the merengue rhythm. The tambora is played sideways with both hands, one with a stick, the other without. Downbeats are played with the hand, while the stick plays the syncopations; both play different open drum figures. Congas are now used along with tambora in dance bands. A metal torpedo-shaped guiro, called *guira,* played with a metal scraper, is also used in merengue.

Although clave is not played with merengue the rhythm fits over 3-2 clave.

FIRST SECTION: MERENGUE

This pattern uses the floor tom, floor tom rim and snare drum cross-stick, playing the tambora patterns. The left hand (snare drum cross stick) imitates what is played on one side of the tambora, while the right hand imitates what is played on the other head and wood around the head.

Exercise 1 First part of merengue rhythm, merengue pattern

SECOND SECTION: JALEO

Now let's hear the second part, called jaleo.

Exercise 2 Second part of merengue rhythm, jaleo pattern

THIRD SECTION: APANPICHO

Last is the third part or swing section, called apanpicho. In this section, the bass goes from a "2 feel" (playing on "1" and "3") to a syncopated bass line similar to that played in son music.

Exercise 3   Third section or swing section of merengue rhythm, called apanpicho

MERENGUE, FULL DRUMSET

Merengue can be played on drumset. The bass drum usually plays downbeats, the hi-hat plays the guira part and the tambora (the jaleo pattern is most often used) is played on floor tom, floor tom rim and snare drum cross-stick.

Exercise 4   Merengue, full drumset

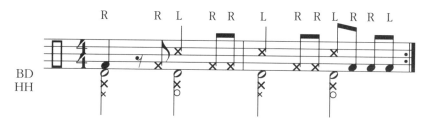

When you listen to merengue, notice that the bass will play in a "2 feel" most of the time and will sometimes go to a syncopated feel like the basic pattern played in son music (usually on the third section, apanpicho).

MERENGUE-SONGO PATTERN

Here's an interesting mixture of merengue and songo. Remember we said that merengue is basically a 3-2 pattern. This is part of the apanpicho pattern (on the 3-part of the clave) mixed with the first bar of the basic songo pattern (over the 2-part of the clave).

Exercise 5   Merengue-songo

54

SECTION 10
TWO PATTERNS BY FRANK MALABE

The next two examples are patterns created for the drumset by Frank Malabe. These patterns are not based on any one rhythm, they are created from different Afro-Cuban rhythms.

"IRVING BLUES"

Exercise 1 *"Irving Blues"*

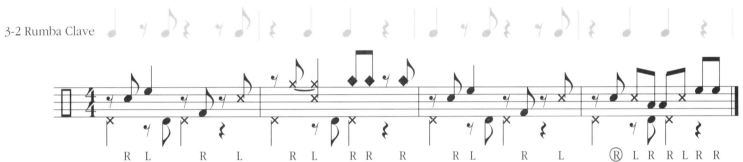

3-2 Rumba Clave

R L   R   L   R L R R R R   R L   R   L   ℝ L R R L R R

"RUMBA IYESA"

This next pattern uses phrases heard in **bata** drumming (the drumming of the Yoruba religion known as *Santeria*, which is practiced in Cuba and New York). This example is played on two drumsets because bata drumming involves three different-sized double-headed drums.

Exercise 2 "Rumba Iyesa"

Drumset 1

2-3 Rumba Clave

HH

L   R   L   R   R

Drumset 2

R L R   R   L

SECTION 11
MEDLEY OF PLAYING EXAMPLES

The tape ends with a medley of some of the rhythms we've covered. You'll hear 16 bars of each pattern with breaks in between.

Section 11, A medley of playing examples; Example 1 with drumset, conga and clave

In the next example you'll hear only conga and clave so you can try the drumset part. Clave continues through the entire medley, changing phrasing in some of the different sections. Use the clave as a reference when going from one pattern to another. Use the chart for the drumset patterns and breaks.

Example 2 with no drumset, only conga and clave

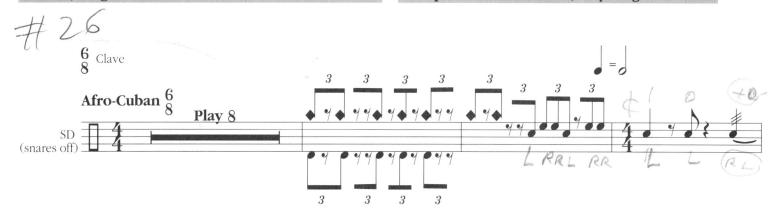

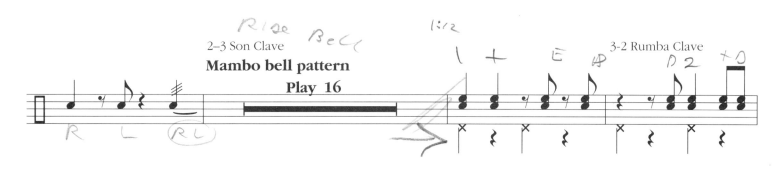

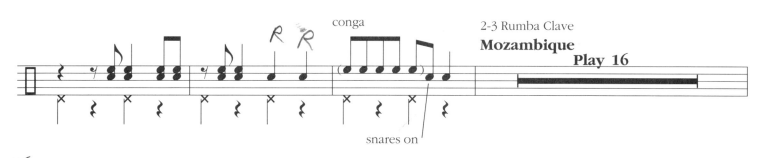

57

GLOSSARY

ABAKWA (ab-ah-KWAH) A secret male society in Cuba.

ABANICO (ab-ah-NEE-koh) Timbale figure used to set up figures and open and close sections. Spanish word for fan.

APANPICHAO (ah-PAHN-pee-chow) The third or "swing" section of the merengue rhythm.

BATA (bah-TAH) The sacred hourglass-shaped drums of the Yoruba of Nigeria and the Santeria religion of Cuba and the U.S.

BEMBE (bem-BEH) A West African rhythm originating from religious gatherings that feature drumming, singing and dancing.

BOMBA (BOHM-bah) A Puerto Rican dance of strong African influence.

BOLERO (boh-LEH-roh) A lush musical form with romantic lyrics.

BONGO (bohn-GOH) A small double drum used by early guitar and rhythm groups. In salsa, the bongo plays an improvisational counterpoint to the main rhythm.

BONGOCERO (bohn-goh-SEH-roh) Bongo player.

CAJONES (kah-HO-ness) Boxes played in the rumba yambu, also known as *cajas*.

CAMPANA (cahm-PAH-nah) Name for the bell played by the bongocero; also called a bongo bell.

CAMPESINOS (cahm-peh-SEE-nos) The peasants of Cuba, also called *guajiros*.

CARNAVAL (kar-nah-VAHL) The week-long celebration before the start of the Christian Lent season, with music, dancing, and costumes. Known in the U.S. as Mardi Gras. (Spanish spelling)

CASCARA (KAHS-kah-rah) Spanish for "shell," referring to the rhythm that is played on the shell of the timbale.

CHA-CHA-CHA A music and dance form developed by the Cuban charangas from the danzon.

CHARANGA (cha-RANG-gah) The European-style small orchestra of Cuba, consisting of flutes backed by violins and rhythm.

CLAVE (KLAH-vay) The 3-2 or 2-3 rhythmic pattern which is the base of all musical arrangements in Afro-Cuban music. The rhythm is often played with two wooden sticks called *claves*, but whether played or not, it is implied throughout the music.

COLUMBIA (koh-LOOM-bee-yah) Style of rumba played in 6/8 and sung with a combination of Spanish and African phrases.

COMPARSA (kohm-PAR-sah) Parade, especially the parade during Carnaval.

CONGA (KOHN-ga) A group dance of African roots, developed mainly in Cuba but popular in many Latin-American countries. Its rhythm is also called *conga*, and it is played and danced during Carnaval in Cuba.

CONGAS (KOHN-gas) Drums of Congolese origin first used by certain religious groups,but now common to Latin music. See *tumbadora*.

CONGUERO (kohn-GAY-roh) Conga (tumbadora) player.

CONJUNTO (kohn-HOON-toh) The name for various Afro-Cuban brass and percussion ensembles.

CONTRADANZA (kohn-tra-DAHN-sah) A European predecessor of many Latin-American dance forms, performed by two or more couples.

58

CUATRO	(KWAH-troh)	An adaptation of the Spanish guitar having 4 sets of 2 strings. The cuatro is used primarily in Puerto Rican folk music.
DANZA	(DAHN-sah)	A Puerto Rican music and dance form developed from the contradanza. Its Cuban counterpart was the danzon.
DANZON	(dahn-SOHN)	A European-influenced ballroom dance played by the Cuban charangas.
EL BARRIO	(el BAH-ree-oh)	The name for districts or neighborhoods in Latin-American cities. Many Hispanic communities in the U.S. have adopted the name, but it usually refers to Spanish (East) Harlem in New York.
GUA-GUA	(GWAH-gwah)	Mounted piece of bamboo on which the palito patterns are played.
GUAGUANCO	(gwa-wahn-KOH)	One of the African-rooted drum rumbas of Cuba. See *Rumba*.
GUAJIRA	(gwa-HEAR-ah)	The nostalgic music of the Cuban peasants. It has a strong Spanish influence and was originally accompanied by the tres.
GUARACHA	(gwa-RAH-cha)	A song form consisting of a short introduction followed by a faster section. The guaracha is sung by solo and chorus vocals, and originated from satirical Cuban folksongs.
GUIRO	(GWEE-roh)	A "scraper" used to provide rhythm in many Latin American musical styles. It consists of a notched gourd played with a short stick or metal pick. The Dominican version, called *guira*, is made of metal.
HABANERA	(ah-bahn-AY-rah)	A Spanish-derived Cuban dance which became popular at the end of the 19th century. It is the ancestor of the tango and other dances.
JALEO	(ha-LAY-oh)	Second section of the merengue pattern.
LATIN/JAZZ		Originally a pairing of the Cuban rhythm section with the brass and reeds of jazz. Eventually, other elements of both styles were added.
MAMBO	(MAHM-boh)	A repeating instrumental section of a song, also known as *montuno*. It is often mistaken for a specific type of rhythm or song form. The dance done during this part of the music also became known as the mambo.
MARACAS	(mah-RAH-cas)	A pair of rattles filled with dried seeds or pebbles, used to provide rhythmic counterpoint.
MERENGUE	(meh-REHN-geh)	A brisk dance from the Dominican Republic.
MOZAMBIQUE	(moh-zahm-BEE-kay)	Rhythm originating in the conga rhythm, made popular first in Cuba and later in New York.
QUINTO	(KEEN-toh)	High-pitched conga drum, used primarily as a solo instrument in rumba guaguanco.
PALITO	(pah-LEE-toh)	Rhythmic patterns that are played along with the clave when playing rumbas; also, the sticks used to play these patterns.
PLENA	(PLEH-nah)	A Puerto Rican song form of strong African influence. Later forms made use of the Spanish guitar.
RUMBA	(ROOM-bah)	The secular drum and voice music of urban Cuba. Variations include the columbia, the guaguanco, and the yambu. This form consists of African-based drumming, singing, and dancing with mostly Spanish vocals. The rumba (or rhumba) of the '30s dance craze is closer in style to a *bolero*.
SANTERIA	(sahn-teh-REE-ah)	The African Yoruba religion, as it has survived in Cuba.
SALIDOR	(sahl-ee-DOR)	Low-pitched conga drum played in the rumba guaguanco.

SALSA	(SAHL-sah)	A generic term for a kind of Afro-Cuban-based music with vocals, usually influenced by other Caribbean styles and by jazz. The word first came into use in New York City to describe a particular hybrid-Latin music style.
SHEKERE	(SHAY-keh-reh)	An African-derived percussion instrument made of a gourd with a net of beads covering the outside.
SON	(sohn)	One of the oldest Afro-Cuban musical forms, balancing both its Spanish and African elements.
TAMBORA	(tahm-BOH-rah)	Double-headed drum used in the merengue rhythm.
TIMBALES	(teem-BAH-less)	Derived from the kettle drums (or timpani), timbales are two metal drums, a cowbell, and often a cymbal. Used mainly by the charangas before the 1940s, today they are one of the main instruments of salsa.
TIPICO	(TEE-pee-coh)	The older traditional or folk styles of Latin music.
TRES	(trayss)	One of the many adaptations of the Spanish guitar by Latin Americans. The tres, of Cuban origin, has nine strings (3 sets of triple strings).
TRES GOLPES	(trayss GOHL-pays)	Name of both the middle drum and the part it plays in rumba guaguanco.
TUMBADORA	(toom-bah-DOR-ah)	The correct name for the large, single-headed African drum commonly known as the conga.
YAMBU	(yahm-BOO)	One of the three most popular forms of Cuban rumba.
YORUBA	(yo-ROO-bah)	A West African tribe from which many slaves were taken to the Americas.

AFRO-CUBAN SACRED MUSIC (SANTERIA)

Cardona, Milton, *Bembe*. American Clave 1004.

Cuba—Les Danses des Dieux (Compact disc). Ocora C559051. (Field recordings of the music of different religious traditions in Cuba, and some rumba.)

Cult Music of Cuba. Folkways 4410.

Francisco Aguabella y su Tambores Bata, *Santeria—Oro Cantado con Tambores Bata*. GO Productions 10032. (3 audio-cassettes, available from Blue Jay Mercannu, 6821 Tujunga Ave., North Hollywood, CA 91695, telephone (818) 761-2934.)

Grupo Folklorico de Cuba, *Toques y Cantos de Santos, Vol. 1 and 2*. Cubilandia 511 and 512.

The World Music Institute Presents: Cuban and Puerto Rican Music from the African and Hispanic Traditions (Audiocassette tape - side 1 features Orlando "Puntilla" Rios y Nueva Generacion. Available from the World Music Institute; see Bibliography - Resource Centers.)

Puntilla, *Puntilla from La Habana to New York*. Puntilla Records AF101-A/AF101-B.

Rodriguez, Giraldo, *Afro-Ritmos Afro-Cubanos con Los Autenticos Tambores Bata de Giraldo Rodriguez*. Orfeon 12-38008.

AFRO-CUBAN FOLKLORIC MUSIC (BEMBE, CONGA, ETC.)

Antologia de la Musica Afro-Cubana Vol. 6, Fiesta de Bembe. Areito LD-3997.

Caliente—Puerto Rican and Cuban Expression in New York. New World Records NW 244. (Produced by Rene Lopez)

Grupo Afro-Cubano dirigido por Alberto Zayas, *Afro-Frenetic: Tambores de Cuba—Cuban Afro Folklore Rhythms*, Panart LP-3053.

Grupo Folklorico y Experimental Nuevayoriquino, *Concepts in Unity*. Salsoul SAL 2-400 series.

Grupo Folklorico y Experimental Nuevayoriquino, *Lo Dice Todo*. Salsoul SAL-4110. (Produced by Rene Lopez)

Puente, Tito, *Top Percussion*. Racano (RCA) DKL 1-3175.

Santamaria, Mongo, *Drums and Chants*. Vaya JMVS 56 - series 0698.

Santamaria, Mongo, *Yambu*. Fantasy 3267 (reissued in *Afro-Roots*, Prestige 24018).

RUMBA (GUAGUANCO)

El Grupo Folklorico de Alberto Zayas, *Guaguanco Afro-Cubano: El Vive Bien con el Grupo Folklorico de Alberto Zayas*. Panart LP-2055.

Los Munequitos de Matanzas, *Guaguanco, Columbia, Yambu*. Siboney LD 227.

Los Papines, *El Retorno a la Semilla*. Color 102-35109.

Papin y sus Rumberos (Los Papines), *Guaguanco—Conjunto Guaguanco Matancero*. Antilla 565.

Valdez, Patato, and Totico, *Patato y Totico* (with Arsenio Rodriguez on tres and Cachao on bass). RVC 1102.

CARNAVAL (CONGA)

Grupo Afro-Cubano, *Congas y Comparsas—Carnaval Habanero*. Cubilandia 512.

Grand Carnavals d'Amerique (de Rio a Quebec) (Compact disc). Playa Sound PS-65008. (A compilation of different musical carnival traditions including examples from Cuba, Brazil, New Orleans, and much of the Caribbean and South America. Available from the World Music Institute—see Bibliography - Resource Centers.)

SON—EARLY STYLE (CUBA, 1920's, 30's)

La Historia de Son Cubano—The Roots of Salsa, Vol. 1—Sexteto Bolona, Folklyric records 9053; *Vol. 2—Sexteto Habanera*, Folkloric records 9054 (Distributed by Arhoolie Records).

Sexteto Habanera, *Collecion de Oro* (Compact disc). CD 1201.

Septeto National de Ignacio Pineiro, *Recordando al Septeto National*. Esquivel LP-004.

Septeto National de Ignacio Pineiro, *Bienvenido Granda con el Septeto National*. Memorias LP-586.

CONJUNTO STYLE (1940's, 50's, 60's)

Chappotin, Felix, *Mi Son, Mi Son, Mi Son—Canta Miguelito Cuni y Ignacio Carrillo*. Barbaro B 201.

Conjunto Casino, *A Bailar con el Conjunto Casino*. Panart 2006.

Conjunto Casino, *Conjunto Casino*. Ansonia ALP 1258.

Rodriguez, Arsenio, *Arsenio Rodriguez y su Conjunto*. Ansonia ALP-1337.

Rodriguez, Arsenio, *Exitos*. Tropical 5005.

Rodriguez, Arsenio, *Sabroso y Caliente*. Puchito MLP 586.

POPULAR SON STYLE (CUBA, 1940's, 50's)

More, Beny, *Asi es Beny*. Discuba LPD 541.

More, Beny, *El Inigualable*. Discuba LPD 531.

Pozo, Chano and Arsenio Rodriguez, *Legends of Afro-Cuban Music*. (Chano Pozo with the Arsenio Rodriguez and Machito orchestras.) Pro-Artes, Artes Hispanicos, Spanish Music Center, Inc., SMC-1152.

Sonora Matancera, *Sonora Matancera, Canta: Bienvenido Granda*. Ansonia ALP-1225.

DANCE ORCHESTRAS (NEW YORK CITY, 1950's, 60's)

Machito and his Afro-Cubans, *Dance Date with Machito*. Palladium PLP-111.

Machito and his Afro-Cubans, *Machito Plays Mambo and Cha-Cha-Cha*. Palladium PLP-109.

Puente, Tito, *Dance Mania* (reissued on compact disc). RCA International 7252RL.

Puente, Tito, *Mamborama—Tito Puente, King of the Cha-Cha Mambo and His Orchestra*. Palladium PLP-100.

Rodriguez, Tito, *Tito Rodriguez at the Palladium*. Palladium PLP-108.

CHARANGA (CUBA)

Orquesta Aragon, *Cojale con la Orquesta Aragon*. Discuba LPD-502.

Orquesta Aragon, *Me Voy Para La Luna*. Discuba LPD-520.

Fajardo, Jose, *Fajardo y sus Estrellas*. Panart LPP 3147.

Fajardo, Jose, *Saludos from Fajardo*. Panart 3058.

CHARANGA (NEW YORK CITY)

Orquesta Broadway, *Pasaporte*. Coco CLP-126.

Orquesta Broadway, *Esta Pegando*. West Side Latino WSLA-4069.

Pacheco, Johnny, *Pacheco y su Charanga, Vols. 1,2 & 3*. Alegre LPA-801, 805, 811.

Palmieri, Charlie, *Charanga Duboney: Echoes of an Era*. West Side Latino WSLA-240-1.

Santamaria, Mongo, *Sabroso!* Original Jazz Classics OJC-281 (reissue: Fantasy 8058).

LATIN JAZZ (1940's, 50's, 60's)

Machito, *Afro-Cuban Jazz* (with Chico O'Farrill, Charlie Parker, Dizzy Gillespie). Verve VE-2-2522.

Machito, *Flute to Boot* (Machito and His Big Band). TTH Records TTH-1905.

Machito, *Kenya.* Palladium PLP-104.

Santamaria, Mongo, *Greatest Hits.* Fantasy MPF-4529.

Santamaria, Mongo, *Watermelon Man.* Milestone M-47012.

Tjader, Cal, *Mambo with Cal Tjader.* Original Jazz Classics OJC-271 (reissue - Fantasy 3202).

Tjader, Cal *Tjader plays Mambo.* Original Jazz Classics OJC-274 (reissue - Fantasy 3221).

Rodriguez, Tito, *Live at Birdland (with Jazz Soloists: Zoot Sims, Clark Terry, Bobbie Brookmeyer, Al Cohn, Bernie Leighton).* Palladium PLP-102.

POPULAR BANDS (CUBA, 1960's, 70's)

Sonora Matancera, *50 Anos de la Sonora Matancera, Vol. 1,* Seeco SSD-4002; *Vol. 2,* SSD-4003.

Sonora Matancera, *Sonora Matancera—Ismael Miranda.* Fania JM-632.

POPULAR BANDS (PUERTO RICO, 1960's, 70's, 80's)

El Gran Combo, *Smile.* Gema LPG5-3078

El Gran Combo, *Today, Tomorrow, and Always—25th Anniversary.* Combo RCSLP 2050-3, series 2498.

Rosario, Willie, *Nuevos Horizontes.* Bronco 128.

Sonora Poncena, *Back to Work.* INCA (No serial number).

POPULAR BANDS—SALSA (NEW YORK CITY, 1960's, 70's, 80's)

Cruz, Celia and Johnny Pacheco, *Celia and Johnny.* Vaya JMVS-84, series 0798.

Cruz, Celia, *Son con Guaguanco.* Tico 1143.

Barretto, Ray, *Aqui Se Puede.* JM-642.

Barretto, Ray, *Barretto Live—Tomorrow* (2 records with timbale solos by Jimmy Delgado, Tito Puente, and Orestes Vilato). Atlantic SD-2509.

Blades, Ruben and Willie Colon, *Siembre.* Fania JMOO-537, series 0798.

Colon, Willie, *Cosa Nuestra.* Fania SLP-384.

Harlow, Larry, *Tribute to Arsenio Rodriguez.* Fania SLP-00404.

Harlow, Larry, *Senor Salsa* (with Frank Malabe and Louis Bauzo). Tropical Buddha TBLP-007.

Oquendo, Manny y su Conjunto Libre, *Ritmo, Sonido, Estilo.* Montuno MLP-522.

Ortiz, Luis "Perico," *Super Salsa.* New Generation Records NG 710.

Palmieri, Charlie, *A Giant Step* (with Frank Malabe). Tropical Buddha TBLP-003.

Palmieri, Eddie, *Azucar (Sugar for You).* Tico SLP-1122.

Palmieri, Eddie, *Molasses.* Tico LP-148.

Palmieri, Eddie, *Sentido.* Coco CLP 103.

MOZAMBIQUE

Palmieri, Eddie, *Mambo con Conga is Mozambique.* Tico SCLP-1126.

DESCARGAS ("JAM SESSIONS," CUBA)

Cachao y su Ritmo Caliente, *Cuban Jam Sessions in Miniature—Descargas* (with the great conguero Tata Guines). Panart 102-28037.

Cuban Jam Session, Under the Direction of Julio Gutierrez, Vol. 1, Panart 102-28041; *Vol. 2,* Panart 102-28042.

Cuban Jam Session, Under the Direction of Nino Rivera, Vol. 3. Panart 102-28044.

DESCARGAS (NEW YORK CITY)

Descargas at the Village Gate, Vol. 1. Tico LP-1135.

Fania All-Stars, *Fania All-Stars Live at Yankee Stadium.* Fania series 0598, XSLP-00476.

Puente, Tito, *Puente in Percussion* (with Mongo Santamaria, Willie Bobo, and "Patato" Valdez). Tico series 0698, LPS-88993.

Tico All-Stars, Vol. 2. Tico LP-1145.

CONTEMPORARY GROUPS (CUBA, 1970's, 80's)

Irakere, *Chekere Son.* Milestone M-9103.

Irakere, *Tierra en Trance.* Areito LPS-94-856.

Los Van Van, *Al Son del Caribe* (with Changuito on timbales). Areito (COLOR) 102-35121.

Los Van Van, *Songo* (with Changuito). Mango Records MLPS-9825.

Rubalcaba, Gonzalo, *Grupo Proyecto de Gonzalo Rubalcaba.* Areito LD-4235 (Adventurous and creative "Afro-Cuban fusion.")

CONTEMPORARY GROUPS (PUERTO RICO, 1970's, 80's)

Batacumbele, *Afro-Cuban Jazz—Angel "Cachete" Maldonaldo y su Grupo.* Montuno MLJ-525.

Batacumbele, *En Aquellos Tiempos.* Tierrazo TLP-011. (One of the most original and creative albums of Afro-Cuban fusion, and very well recorded.)

Batacumbele, *Con un Poco de Songo.* Tierrazo Records 1981.

Zaperoko, *Cosa de Locos.* Montuno 519.

Zaperoko, *Zaperoko II.* Montuno 523.

CONTEMPORARY GROUPS (NEW YORK CITY, 1970's, 80's)

Barretto, Ray, *The Other Road.* Fania SLP-0048.

Blades, Ruben, *Buscando America.* Elektra/Asylum 60352.

Gonzalez, Jerry, *Ya Yo Me Cure.* Pangaea (IRS records) PAN Line 6242.

Gonzalez, Jerry and the Fort Apache Band, *The River is Deep* Enja 4040.

Gonzalez, Jerry, *Rumba Para Monk* (Compact disc). Sunnyside SSC-1036 D.

Palmieri, Eddie, *The Sun of Latin Music.* Coco CLP 109XX.

PUERTO RICAN FOLKLORIC AND DANCE MUSIC (JIBARO, BOMBA, PLENA)

Caliente —Puerto Rican and Cuban Expression in New York. New World Records NW-244.

Canario y su Grupo, *Plenas.* Ansonia ACP-1232.

Cortijo, Rafael, *Cortijo y su Combo—Bombas para Bailar.* Tropical TRLP-5172.

The World Music Institute Presents: Cuban and Puerto Rican Music from the African and Hispanic Traditions. World Music Institute; see Bibliography - Resource Centers. (Side 2 features Puerto Rican folkloric music.)

MERENGUE (DOMINICAN REPUBLIC, NEW YORK CITY)

Vargas, Wilfrido, *Wilfrido Vargas.* Karen KLP-14

Viloria, Angel, Dioris Valladares and Ramon Garcia, *Merengues.* Ansonia Records (Compact disc) HGCD 1206. (Good examples of early folkloric and urban merengues.)

Also see recordings by Johnny Ventura, and Millie y Los Vecinos.

(BOOKS, FILMS, VIDEOS, AND RESOURCE CENTERS, COMPILED BY JOHN GRAY. ©1989)

AFRICA

Chernoff, John, *African Rhythm and African Sensibility.* Chicago: University of Chicago Press, 1979. 261p.

Graham, Ronnie, *The Da Capo Guide to Contemporary African Music.* New York: Da Capo Press, 1988. 315p. A comprehensive discographical and geographical survey of contemporary African pop music styles.

THE CARIBBEAN AND LATIN AMERICA
Books and Articles

Manuel, Peter, "Latin America and the Caribbean," *Popular Musics of the Non-Western World.* New York: Oxford University Press, 1988, pp. 24-83.

Roberts, John Storm, *Black Music of Two Worlds.* New York: Morrow Paperbacks, 1974. 282p.

Journals

The Beat. Bi-monthly, formerly *The Reggae & African Beat.* "World Beat" magazine covering popular music styles being recorded and performed around the world today. (Bongo Productions, P.O. Box 29820, Los Angeles, CA 90029).

Bibliographies

De Lerma, Dominique-Rene, *Bibliography of Black Music, Vol. 3: Geographical Studies.* Westport, CT: Greenwood Press, 1982. ("The Caribbean," pp. 127-163).

AFRO-CUBAN SACRED AND FOLKLORIC MUSIC
Books

Murphy, Joseph M., *Santeria: An African Religion in America.* Boston: Beacon Press, 1988. 189p. Excellent brief introduction to Santeria, the Afro-Cuban religion, as practiced in the Bronx.

Ortiz, Fernando, *La Africania de la Musica Folklorica de Cuba.* 2nd ed., revised. Havana: Editora Universitaria, 1965. 489p. (Orig. 1952, Spanish text)

Ortiz, Fernando, *Los Instrumentos de la Musica Afrocubana.* Havana: Ediciones del Ministerio de Educacion de Cuba, 1952-1955. 5 vols. (Spanish text)

Ortiz, Fernando, *La Musica Afrocubana.* Madrid: Ediciones Jucar, 1975. 339p. (Spanish text)

These three works by Fernando Ortiz remain the most detailed and accurate portrait yet offered on Afro-Cuban folkloric and religious music, although they are difficult to find.

Articles

Wentz, Brook, "Cuban Rites: Drummer Milton Cardona," *Option: Music Alternatives* (November-December 1986), pp. 37-39. Interview with New York-based Santero and bata drummer Milton Cardona.

AFRO-CUBAN POPULAR MUSIC
Books

Aros, Andrew A., *The Latin Music Handbook.* Diamond Bar, CA: Applause Publications, 1978. 103p. Brief historical and discographical overview of a variety of popular Latin music styles, including salsa.

Brown, Thomas A., *Afro-Latin Rhythm Dictionary.* Van Nuys, CA: Alfred Publishing Co., 1984. 48p. (Alfred Handy Guide #2427, available from Alfred Publishing, 16380 Roscoe Blvd., Van Nuys, CA 91410-0003.)

Gerard, Charley with Marty Sheller, *Salsa: The Rhythm of Latin Music.* Crown Point, IN: White Cliffs Media Co., 1989. 137p.

Roberts, John Storm, *The Latin Tinge: The Impact of Latin American Music on the United States.* New York: Original Music, 1985. 246p. (Reprint of 1979 edition).

Roldon, C.M., *El Libro de la Salsa: Cronica de la Musica del Caribe Urbano.* Caracas, Venezuela, 1980. 340p. (Spanish text)

Orovio, Helio, *Diccionario de la Musica Cubana—Biografico y Tecnico.* Havana, Cuba: 1981. (Published by Editorial Letras Cubanas, Calle G, No. 505, El Vadad, Cuidad de la Habana, Cuba.) Biographies of the great musicians of Afro-Cuban and Cuban music.

Books with Sections on Afro-Cuban Popular Music

Leymarie, Isabelle, "Salsa and Latin Jazz," *Hot Sauces: Latin and Caribbean Pop,* edited by Billy Bergman. New York: Quill/Morrow, 1985, pp. 96-115.

Marre, Jeremy, and Hannah Charlton, "Salsa! Latin Music of New York and Puerto Rico," *Beats of the Heart: Popular Music of the World.* New York: Pantheon, 1986, pp. 70-81. This is the written accompaniment to a video of the same name. (See Media Materials section)

Journals

Latin N.Y. All issues. Izzy Sanabria, editor. The primary source for information on New York salsa and merengue of the 1970s and early 80's.

Articles

Barr, W.L., "The Salsa Rhythm Section," *Educator,* Vol. 12, No. 2 (1978-80): pp. 15-18.

Crook, Larry, "A Musical Analysis of the Cuban Rumba," *Latin American Research Review.* Vol. 3, No. 1 (1982): pp. 92-123.

Manuel, Peter, "The Anticipated Bass in Cuban Popular Music" *Latin American Music Review,* Vol. 6, No. 2 (1985): pp. 249-261.

Singer, Roberta L, "Tradition and Innovation in Contemporary Latin Popular Music in New York City," *Latin American Music Review,* Vol. 4, No. 2 (Fall/Winter 1983): pp. 183-202.

Thompson, Robert Farris, "Portrait of the Pachanga: The Music, The Players, The Dancers," *Saturday Review* (October 28, 1961): pp. 42-43, 54. Brief discussion of the Afro-Cuban dance of the early 1960's, its Yoruba sources, etc.

Santos, John, Liner notes to the LP "Sexteto Bolona, La Historia del Son Cubano—The Roots of Salsa, Vol. 1." Folklyric Records 9053 (distributed by Arhoolie Records). A good early history of the Cuban son.

Media Materials (Videos, Films, Audiotapes)

Beats of the Heart: Salsa. Directed by Jeremy Marre. Includes performances, interviews, and recording sessions with such stars as Celia Cruz, Tito Puente, Ruben Blades, Charlie Palmieri, Ray Barretto and more. (Available from Shanachie Records, P.O. Box 208, Newton, NJ 07860.)

Crossover Dreams (1985). Directed by Leon Ichaso. Features Ruben Blades as a salsa musician trying to get out of the cuchifrito circuit to make it as a major recording artist. (Available from New Yorker Films, 16 W. 61st Street, New York, NY 10023, tel. 212/247-6110).

Drums Across the Sea (1986). Video, 90 min. Tells how African and Spanish music developed in Cuba and came to the U.S., where it burst on the scene as Afro-Cuban jazz and the dance crazes of the 1940's and 50's, and its current renaissance in popularity as salsa. Features Dizzy Gillespie, Irakere, Ruben Blades, Mongo Santamaria and others. (Available from Cultural Research and Communication, c/o Lion's Gate Studio, 1861 South Bundy Drive, Los Angeles, CA 90025.)

Musica. (1985) Directed by Gustavo Paredes. Video, 58 min. (Available from Latin American Music in Alternative Spaces, P.O. Box 2207, New York, NY 10027).

Viva Latino! Part 11—La Musica. Audiotape, 30 minutes. Explains the prominent role of music in the Latino lifestyle and features Afro-Cuban and Puerto Rican music. (Available from

National Public Radio, Cassette Publishing, 2025 M St. NW, Washington, DC 20036. Cassette # SP-80-09-24.)

PUERTO RICO
Articles
Lopez, Rene, "Drumming in the New York Puerto Rican Community: A Personal Account," *Black People and Their Culture: Selected Writings from the African Diaspora,* edited by Linn Shapiro. Washington DC: Smithsonian Institute, Festival of American Folklife, African Diaspora, 1976, pp. 106-109.

THE DOMINICAN REPUBLIC
Books and Articles
Lizardo Barinas, Fradique, *Instrumentos Musicales Indigenas Dominicanos.* Santo Domingo: Alfa y Omega, 1975. 109p. (Spanish text)

Ramon y Rivera, Luis Felipe, "Dominican Republic," *The New Grove Dictionary of Music and Musicians,* Vol.. 5, pp. 535-538.

MAIL ORDER AND RECORD OUTLETS
Bate Records (140 Delancey St., New York NY 10002, tel. 212/677-3180) Extensive Latin selection.

Caravan Music (P.O. Box 49036, Austin TX 78765) Free mail order catalogue. Excellent selection of Latin recordings.

Discoteca Latino-Americano (92-06 168th Place, Jamaica NY 11433)

Original Music (R.D. 1, Box 190, Tivoli NY 12583, tel. 914/756-2767) Free mail-order catalogue. Includes large selection of Latin recordings.

Record Mart, Inc. (Times Square Station, 1470 Broadway, New York NY 10036) One of the best sources of Cuban and Latin recordings.

Down Home Music, Inc. (10341 San Pablo Ave., El Cerrito CA 94530, tel. 415/525-1494) Good source of vintage and ethnic records, plus books and magazines. Free catalog.

RESOURCE CENTERS
Black Arts Research Center (30 Marion St., Nyack NY 10960, tel. 914/358-2089) An archival resource center dedicated to the documentation, preservation, and dissemination of the African cultural legacy, including records, cassettes, videotapes, books, journals and bibliographies.

Caribbean Cultural Center (408 W. 58th St., New York NY 10019, tel. 212/307-7420) A non-profit organization dedicated to the study of African traditions in the arts and culture of the Caribbean and other areas. They sponsor many excellent concerts of African-based folkloric music.

Center for Cuban Studies (124 W. 23rd St., New York NY 10011) A non-profit organization that specializes in Cuban research material, including books, videos, and recordings.

The Harbor Performing Arts Center (1 E. 104th St., New York NY 10029, tel. 212/427-2244 x 572) Excellent classes in Afro-Cuban and Puerto Rican folkloric and popular drumming by some of the great drummers of these traditions; also instruction on other instruments, ensembles, and dance traditions.

World Music Institute (109 W. 27th St., New York NY 10011, tel. 212/206-1050) A non-profit organization which presents concerts in traditional and contemporary music from around the world. They house a fine collection of records, tapes, CDs, and literature on world music.

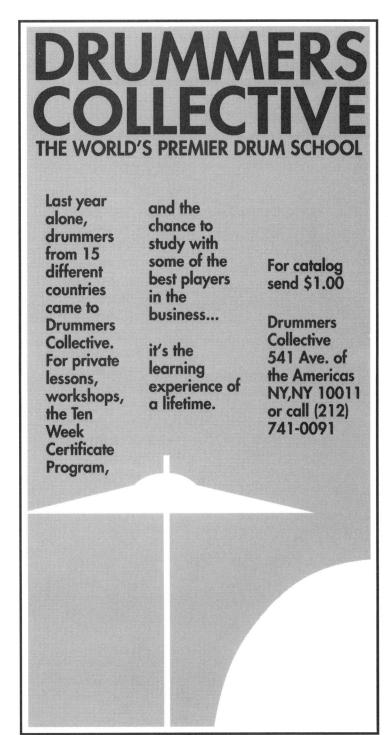